SELF EFFICACY AND QUALITY OF LIFE AS THE INFLUENCING FACTORS FOR WOMEN ENTREPRENEURS AND BUSINESS SUCCESS:

THE CASE OF SMALL SCALE INDUSTRY IN ANDHRA PRADESH STATE.

Dr. Charith Venkat Pidikiti

Alpha-X Publications

Charith Venkat Pidikiti asserts the moral right to be identified as the author of this work.

Paperback: **ISBN-10:** 3982187001

ISBN-13: 978-3982187006

E-Book: ASIN: B0863ZL2ZT

Cover concept and Design by Alpha-X

Published by Alpha-X

Author

Charith is a 1986 born, globetrotter and a biomedical engineer, who currently lives in Munich, Germany. A true jack-of-all-trades who religiously follows four words, "Ambition has no limits". Apart from being a full time employee at a Fortune 500 company, he is also an entrepreneur, an artist, a drummer, a fitness aficionado and a writer, who loves and collects classic cars and history books.

Hailing from India, a country rich in diverse religions and varied cultures, he was always obsessed with history, mythology and religion, yet it was his penchant for science since a young age that led him to study at the New York University, in one of the largest cosmopolitan cities of the world, NYC. After which he moved to work in Germany, where he is currently working on his Doctorate, has accomplished over four medical and two business publications and won the "Making A Difference" Award.

He constantly travels around the world with curiosity, learning foreign traditions, cultures, religions, modern technology or simply in pursuit of new experiences.

Follow the Author:

https://instagram.com/charithvenkat

https://www.facebook.com/charith.venkat

ACKNOWLEDGEMENTS

I was born in a relatively small town called Vijayawada in India, but blessed with two highly motivated parents, my role models, each excelling in the field of Entrepreneurship and Pediatrics respectively, but their qualifications go beyond their doctorates. They too spread out in multiple business directions such as real estate, property development and media. My mother is the founding member of the world-renowned social organization called *"Association of Lady Entrepreneurs of India"*, with a mission to help underprivileged-women become successful business-women and entrepreneurs, through education, training and access to finance. ALEAP now has a global footprint and has even achieved the prestigious "Green-Tech Award", for its solutions on waste management and also an award for contribution towards the *"Ministry of Micro, Small & Medium Enterprises sector"*.

Like most people from a third-world country, they started from humble beginnings and struggling backgrounds but they reached great heights and recognition through hard work and dedication. Most importantly, my parents and their experiences have helped me start from a much higher step; since I was able to avoid, the trials and errors they have encountered and created my own assessments. However to top it all off, the one thing they ever-so-lovingly stressed upon is *„to give back to the society and the world as well"*, this was something they learnt from their journey and wanted to propagate through me as well. Learn, earn, succeed so you can provide to the underprivileged, and I have seen the struggles of the underprivileged women in India. I consider it my responsibility to contribute and give back to them, to use what I have learnt to bring them out of their struggles.

ABSTRACT

"The true entrepreneur is a doer, not a dreamer" - when Nolan Bushnell first said those words, they resonated deep within me. Not only do I agree with those words, I follow. Being a full-time employee was no excuse from using the other 10 hours of my day, so I started multiple part-time businesses, ranging from Exotic-Car-Rentals, Online-Webinars to Cryptocurrency and even spanning out to writing and marketing my own historical-fiction book, which is currently undergoing evaluation by leading publishers. However, time and resources are limited for all. We need the experience, knowledge and expertise of each other to symbiotically advance towards our goals. Mistakes happen and we learn, but that experience should also help others (Aspiring Women Entrepreneurs) avoid the same mistakes, and we achieve optimal risk-management. Time and resources will thus, be conserved.

During my time as a student I volunteered for ALEAP (Association of Lady Entrepreneurs of India) and one of my major projects at that time was the famous „Movie on Centre for Entrepreneurship Development - ALEAP" (CED FILM):

During the making of this film I interviewed several members of ALEAP and also the aspiring women entrepreneurs along with the successful ones. It was then I learnt all the hardships and struggles that these women go through on a day-to-day basis and that became an inspiration for me to step up and lend my helping hand.

KEY WORDS

Business

Communication

Development

Engagement

Entrepreneur

Feedback

Management

Media

Medium

Organization

Psychology

Society

Stakeholder

Trends

Women

Contents

CHAPTER ONE

INTRODUCTION

1.1 Background of the Study

Entrepreneurship is a process that determining a potential venture with the limited resource available by an individual. It was part of the world economic system and evolved from century to century. Entrepreneur "known as a management agent" who perform all the functional task. Beyond any doubt, entrepreneurship is an essential activity that contribute to economic growth, productivity, innovation, and employment. According to Hisrich (2005), there are history proved that entrepreneur is the person who exploit opportunities by willing to take risk into account make a significant contribution toward economic growth.

It was additionally demonstrated in the ahead of schedule of 2002s by Christensen et al. that finished up various of inquires about concurred that entrepreneurial exercises are one of the key main thrusts to a country's development. In 2003, Ariff and Abubakar reported that since early 1970s business visionaries become the benefactor as employment maker and improve GDP development.

There are likewise studies that prescribed a chief with expert firm oversee abilities should assume control over the spot of a business person as a leader. However, Willard et al. (2000) found that entrepreneurs could have share similar abilities with proficient administrators in competencies, for example, activity, money related, marketing, human asset, and functional management skills. Conflicting, report of Bruno et al. (2002) draw a consideration on the administrative inadequacy that lead to venture failure.

Be that as it may. As per Casson (2003) despite the fact that there is no standard definition to explain entrepreneurial achievement, however the contribution of entrepreneurial exercises towards the general public is noteworthy. Numerous researchers contended that achievement is something can be catch even business working in a complex and quickly changing condition by recognizing the basic achievement factors (BAFs) for entrepreneur achievement.

In the early of 2001s, researchers, for example, Aldrich and Martinez, and Ucbasaran et al. discovered that the estimation of CSFs for entrepreneurship is confronting the trail that changing from attribute based approaches towards conduct approaches as quality approaches been seen as never again completely clarified the entrepreneur achievement (Gartner 1990; Mitchell et al. 2002). This finding return the study done by Koh (1996) and Lachman et al. (1980) whose reviews demonstrate the person that imparting higher similarity to the personality will have a higher opportunities to turn into a fruitful entrepreneurs.

Through the complex conclusion made over researchers like Baum et al. (2001), Hankinson et al. (1997), Hussin (1997), McClelland (1961), and Olson and Bosserman (1984), aside from personality factors there are additionally environment factors that influence venture performance significantly.

Indian women are considered as a source of power (Shakti) since legendary times. The Hindus worship goddesses as mothers. Be that as it may, as a general rule, women possess a back seat to men to men. In addition, they are adored as mothers, sisters and other social bondages. Numerous writers have envisioned lady's brains as ocean. The upper layers of their brains, similar to those of the ocean, have fierce waves. Be that as it may, profundities are peaceful and thoughtful.

Ladies' psyches are basically enduring and solid. The fact of the matter is recognized by the Bhagvad Geeta wherein Lord Krishna portrays his appearance in the feminine nature of Medha or higher insight.

Regardless of these realities, in conventional Indian culture women rendered inferior status in family chain of importance. The Indian culture thought about ladies as a weaker sex. Such sociological and social conventions and taboos have kept women torpid for a significant long time.

The Sati pratha [woman setting herself fire on the fire of husband] nearly vanished, yet dishonorable occurrences like female feticide keep on occurring in our alleged created society. Women keep on confronting sexual orientation inclination directly from youth. Frequencies of lack of healthy sustenance, school dropout, early marriage, provocation for endowment and so forth, are critical examples. The male female proportion in our nation has likewise become a significant issue of concern nowadays.

It is very common in Indian families that the women take up more obligations in raising children and keeping up home with adoration and love in an obviously better manner. This part of women being the core of the family is being begrudged by westerners since they need such family confirmations. The task of cooperation of different tasks in a much helpful way, without feeling any touch of it, is in effect all around overseen by Indian women in their families. children raising and offering help benefits at home is till today perceived as main duties of an Indian women. The traditional view of women as a homemaker or at the most an assistant in the spouse's occupation is as yet common.

The word Entrepreneur is gotten from the French word "entrepreneur" which means an individual who attempts the task of uniting different assets and oversees them to accomplish wanted outcomes and take some source. Women entrepreneurship in India represents to a gathering of women who are investigating new roads of economic participation. The entry of the women in sorted out business is a genuinely on-going phenomenon. The Government of India has characterized women entrepreneurs dependent on women participation in equity and utilized of a business.

1.1.2. Characteristics of entrepreneurs

Entrepreneurship in a more extensive sense can be depicted as an imaginative and inventive reaction to the environment. Entrepreneur is a innovator who brings something new into the economy, another strategy for creation not yet tried by the involvement with part of maker concerned, an item with which customers are not recognizable or of new market ever exploited. Subsequent to characterizing Entrepreneur, it is appropriate to concentrate on what is entrepreneurship. One who can face up to decision making can figure out how to be an entrepreneur and to carry on entrepreneurially. Entrepreneurship is a behavior rather than personality trait.

Entrepreneurship might be rehearsed by huge and old business units the same. Further it isn't kept to financial organizations. It stretches out to all organizations financial and social and to possession designs: private, open and helpful area ventures.

In practically every one of the meanings of entrepreneurship, there is an understanding that we are discussing a sort of behavior that incorporates stepping up to the plate, arranging and redesigning of social and monetary instruments to turn assets and circumstances to down to earth record and tolerating danger of failure.

As indicated by Verma (1960) while depicting an entrepreneur notices the accompanying attributes of entrepreneurs: Entrepreneur is fiery, creative, alarm to new chances, ready to acclimate to changing conditions and ready to expect dangers engaged with the change.

- He/She is keen on progressing technologically and in improving the quality of product.

- He/She is keen on extending the scale of operations and reinvests acquiring. As indicated by Histrich(1992) portrays entrepreneur's characteristics in three classifications

- Technical skills: Writing, oral correspondence, checking condition, specialized business management, and innovation know how, relational, posting, capacity to compose, arrange building, instructing, being a cooperative person.

- Business Management Skills: Planning and objective setting, basic leadership, human relations, marketing, fund, bookkeeping, the board, control, exchange, venture launch, overseeing development.

- Personal Entrepreneurial Skills: Inner control, discipline, hazard taking, creative, change situated, diligent, visionary pioneer, capacity to oversee change.

Entrepreneurial Development Institute of India at Gandhinagar describes the entrepreneurial competencies as under

- **Initiative**: Entrepreneurs showing this competency embrace an errand even before being asked or compelled to conditions. Such an activity taking capacity impacts effectiveness and gets premise of feasible upper hand.

- **Seeking and Acting on Opportunities**: By their extremely competent nature fruitful Entrepreneurs increase their entrance to assets, openings, account, land and equipment. They have this one of a kind innovative capacity that causes them take advantage of uncommon opportunities.

- **Persistence**: A significant competency that makes all entrepreneurs archive of blessing and persistence. Difficulties don't dampen such a business visionary and he keeps attempting endeavors to rise triumphant out of issues.

- **Information Seeking**: The nearness of competency loans him a deterministic frame of mind. He distinguishes different wellsprings of data and guarantees a persistent data stream so as to amplify the achievement of the organization

- **Concern for High quality of Work**: The essential undertaking of entrepreneur with such a competency is to beat the current norms of greatness. It is his anxiety for high caliber of work that gives him a feeling of fulfillment and accomplishment

1.1.3. FUNCTIONS OF ENTREPRENEURS

A business person is one who does the entire arrangement of exercises of the business. The elements of a business person are co-appointment of the business the executives of the endeavor, chance taking, controlling the venture, development for change, inspiration and other related exercises. He/she needs to respond to new thoughts, requests and adventure the chances. He/she is relied upon to play out the accompanying capacities (Desai, 2003).

- **Assumption of Risk: -** A business person expect every conceivable danger of business remembering potential outcomes of progress for tastes of purchasers, systems of generation and new innovation. A business visionary attempts to lessen the vulnerabilities by his drive, aptitude and practical insight.

- **Business Decisions: -** The business person needs to choose the nature and kind of products to be created. He enters a business that as indicated by his insight is ideally beneficial. He utilizes his abilities and thoughts to take best choices for improvement of his business.

- **Managerial Functions: -** A business visionary figures plans, orchestrates money, buys crude materials, gives generation offices, sorts out deals and expect undertaking of individual the executives. In a huge foundation, paid staff do these capacities.

- **Function of Innovation: -** A business person is the person who considers thoughts for development in quality and amount of business. He constantly stays educated about developments and attempts to apply them at whatever point and at every possible opportunity.

1.1.4. ENTERPRENURSHIP AMONG WOMEN

Business enterprise has been characterized distinctively relying upon and in line with the changing ethos of financial reality. These days, more noteworthy significance is being attributed to ladies business visionaries as a piece of arrangement by government and different organizations. Ladies speak to 50 percent of total populace and record for two third of complete working hours. They got around 10% of the world's salary and claim short of what one percent of the world's benefits. Against this setting, ladies business people need an exceptional treatment as they need to battle against substantial chances and have a place with the biggest impeded gathering in the nation (Vinze, 1987).

Because of industrialization, urbanization and democratization, the ladies in India are moving towards liberation and are looking for productive work in different fields. Besides, in such a transitional stage, intensely stacked with convention, the Indian ladies discover it progressively hard to alter themselves to the double job that they need to play as customary housewives or mother at home front and rival her men people in the field of business and industry. Ladies have equivalent chances and rights as men. In such a circumstance, it is fundamental to distinguish appropriate innovation which will empower the lady to assume her job as a powerful business visionary without upsetting her needs.

The conditions where a lady business visionary needs to work in our general public must get acknowledgment. A portion of the issues looked by ladies are not equivalent to a standard business visionary would confront. In this manner, it is important to consider such factors which just ladies business visionaries need to confront.

1.1.5. NEED FOR WOMEN ENTREPRENUESHIP

Lady business visionary is qualified for important reinforcement backing of particular and experienced people. The requirement for giving legitimate condition to enterprise is of indispensable significance. Alluring characteristics might be created via preparing. To change the social and monetary structure of our nation and to elevate the hindered area of the general public like ladies, more prominent accentuation is required on enterprising advancement.

HR, the two people, of working age establishes the fundamental quality of financial improvement of a country. Ladies structure a significant section of the work power and the financial pretended by them can't be confined from the system of advancement. The job and level of joining of ladies in monetary advancement is constantly a pointer of ladies' financial freedom and economic wellbeing. Soundarapandian (1999) cites the expressions of Pundit Jawaharlal Nehru – "At the point when ladies push ahead, family moves and the town moves and the country moves." Employment gives financial freedom to ladies. Monetary freedom makes ready for societal position. Also, ladies have become a necessary piece of the industrialized society. A lady must enhance the salary of the family through whatever aptitude she has or has obtained. The present inflationary weights warrant ladies to join the male individuals from the family for verifying considerable job.

As indicated by Rani (1996), enterprise is by all accounts perfect for ladies looking for cooperation in the nation's financial advancement due to specific variables. Development of enterprise is viewed as firmly connected to social, social, strict and mental factors.

1.1.6. PROBLEMS OF WOMEN ENTREPRENEURS

The issues that present day working ladies face can be followed back through history to the Neolithic occasions when a division of work previously existed based on sex. In those days additionally, men chased and ladies accumulated roots and organic products. The ladies' ability to conceive an offspring, a limit that men needed, normally gave ladies a conspicuous spot in the early horticultural society. Along these lines, right now ladies and men were at that point doing various types of work, however ladies were not obviously subordinates to men. Ladies are molded with the numerous obligations. They need to be productive specialists and make a decent attempt to satisfy the activity obligations. Simultaneously they need to be great spouses, great moms and better home directors. She needs to keep up her status in the general public and be regarded by different individuals from the family. Her genuineness towards every one of the obligations is itself a reason for inconvenience.

However, the problems of women entrepreneurs can be briefly discussed in following areas:

- **Problems at Work:** The serious issues looked by utilized ladies were accounted for to be substantial outstanding task at hand, sporadic installment, and absence of assurance of work, absence of maternity benefits, medical issues and nonattendance from home. Frequently conceded instalment was the standard component of the working states of ladies. Managers evaded instalments on a few grounds. Businesses are constantly attentive that if ladies were paid wages day by day and effectively, they may not get their guaranteed administrations on the ensuing day.

- **Problems at Home:** Ladies feel that the measure of work they need to embrace in their homes is very exhausting as they need to take care of diverse kinds of works. On the off chance that they need to look for business other than their residential duty, it would mean an enormous weight of work on them. Indian female laborers still work under specific impediments and hardships. One of the most well-known issues looked by a lady is the double job she needs to play on the household front and work place. Especially, the wedded lady working with little kids locate this double duty a reason for extraordinary mental and physical strain. For them the working hours are long-eight hours at the work environment and at any rate four hours at home.

- **Problems with Husbands:** A few men may steadily pull back from work in the event that their spouses are working. They will in general leave every one of the duties of running the house on them. In the first place a lady wouldn't fret, however bit by bit she understands the weight. He generous gives a minimal expenditure on explicit requests and contends that after all she is procuring and that she could run the house individually. In addition he invests wholeheartedly that he isn't fiddling with her dealings. A few ladies regularly grumble that they are misjudged. Because of weariness, they couldn't react to the spouse's sexual needs they might be affirmed to have ill-conceived relations with certain partners or chief. They are insensitively treated, tormented and even beaten. Ladies feel hurt by such mortifying activities of the spouses, particularly when their trustworthiness is addressed.

- **Problems with Children:** At the point when the mother is working, youngsters additionally feel that they are disregarded and not appropriately cared for. They detest offices different youngsters appreciate. They need to give up numerous things and moreover need to do some work at home to support the mother. At the point when the mother is drained and blows up, they believe they are feeling the loss of the mother's affection. They get frustrated. The working mother, feeling remorseful, attempts to remunerate them in different ways. She would bring a few desserts or toys for the youngsters. The kids after some time know the shortcoming of the mother's brain. They start dealing and requesting things from time to time. For whatever length of time that mother can manage, she continues fulfilling their requests. It ruins the kids and misshapes their obligations.

- **Socio-Economic Problem:** For the significant piece of the day the lady is working in the workplace or work place. In the wake of returning she is occupied with house work and her family. She has no time left to keep up relations with neighbors, companions and family members. She can't visit them unreservedly and invest energy with them or go along with them in like manner programs. Indeed, even she can't go to their assistance when they need particularly at time of disease, marriage, passing or different events. They feel hurt and condemn her as getting egotistical because of her income and state that she isn't the main lady to work. The extraordinary lion's share of the working ladies need to handover their pay to their spouses or in-laws. They shouldn't deal with their very own salary. The sum is spent in home administration. At times are not given even pocket cash or the sum to purchase things for keep consistency individual use. She needs to request and is given some cash as an effortlessness allowed to her.

- **Personal Problems:** The working lady has no time left for her own. She needs rest. She needs to think for her issues or future. She needs to peruse and compose, she needs to do a few exercises of her inclinations, or include in imaginative expressions. Now and again she feels to be alone not upset by anyone. There is no leisure time for her .She can't stand to be surly. In every one of these stresses the lady has no time left to take care of her wellbeing. In any case, anyway she needs to deal with her wellbeing to keep her physically fit to work. She needs to take feeding nourishment and appropriate treatment when required. Again because of difficult work and over troubled by obligations she gets into quick maturing impacts. To adapt up to these and keep up her appeal she needs to take help of beautifying agents and excellence parlor.

- **Other Strategic Problems:** The issues looked by ladies can be separated into three significant parts-Project plan, venture execution and task activity (Vinze, 1987). In period of venture definition, ladies frequently get lost while choosing item. The inability to relate the item to claim foundation is another regular blunder in item determination. Poor specialized help, decision of area, nonappearance of market investigation, bogus fixed venture choice and low value base are some other hazardous regions. If there should arise an occurrence of undertaking execution ladies may make wrong hardware, might be misinformed by special offices or the ladies herself may need enterprising skill. In this stage, she may confront issues with showcasing, generation arranging, and working capital or with business enterprise improvement foundations or offices.

1.1.7. WOMEN ENTREPRENEURSHIP DEVELOPMENT IN INDIA

The Indian economy has been seeing an extreme change since mid - 1991, with new approaches of monetary advancement, globalization and privatization started by the Indian Government. India has incredible pioneering potential. At present, ladies contribution in financial exercises is set apart by a low work interest rate, extreme focus in the sloppy division and work in less gifted occupations. Any procedure went for financial advancement will be top-sided without including ladies who establish half of the total populace. Proof has unequivocally settled that innovative soul is anything but a male right. Ladies business enterprise has picked up force over the most recent three decades with the expansion in the quantity of ladies ventures and their substantive commitment to financial development. The modern execution of Asia-Pacific area pushed by Foreign Direct Investment, mechanical developments and produced trades has brought a wide scope of monetary and social chances to ladies business people. In this powerful world, ladies business visionaries are a significant piece of the worldwide mission for supported financial improvement and social progress.

In India, however ladies have assumed a key job in the general public, their pioneering capacity has not been appropriately tapped because of the lower status of ladies in the general public. It is just from the Fifth Five Year Plan (1974-78) onwards that their job has been expressly perceived with a checked move in the methodology from ladies welfare to ladies advancement and strengthening. The improvement of ladies business enterprise has become a significant part of our arrangement needs. A few approaches and projects are being actualized for the improvement of ladies enterprise in India. There is a requirement for changing the outlook towards ladies to give equivalent rights as cherished in the constitution. The advancement towards sexual orientation equity is moderate and is somewhat because of the inability to join cash to strategy duties. In the expressions of president APJ Abdul Kalam "enabling ladies is an essential for making a decent country, when ladies are engaged, society with dependability is guaranteed.

1.1.8. MICRO, SMALL AND MEDIUM ENTERPRISES (MSME)

The President under Notification dated 9th May 2007 has amended the Government of India (Allocation of Business) Rules, 1961. Pursuant to this amendment, Ministry of Agro and Rural Industries (Krishi Evam Gramin Udyog Mantralaya) and Ministry of Small Scale Industries (Laghu Udyog Mantralaya) have been merged into a single Ministry, namely, "MINISTRY OF MICRO, SMALL AND MEDIUM ENTERPRISES (SUKSHMA LAGHU AUR MADHYAM UDYAM MANTRALAYA)".

Around the world, the miniaturized scale little and medium endeavors (MSMEs) have been acknowledged as the motor of monetary development and for advancing even handed improvement. The significant preferred position of the area is its business potential at low capital expense. The work force of the MSME part is a lot higher than that of the enormous undertakings. The MSMEs comprise over 90% of all out endeavors in the vast majority of the economies and are credited with creating the most noteworthy paces of work development and record for a significant portion of modern generation and fares. In India as well, the MSMEs assume an indispensable job in the general mechanical economy of the nation. As of late the MSME area has reliably enrolled higher development rate contrasted with the general mechanical division. With its deftness and dynamism, the segment has demonstrated commendable ingenuity and flexibility to endure the on-going financial downturn and downturn. According to accessible measurements (fourth Census of MSME Sector), this division utilizes an expected 59.7 million people spread over 26.1 million undertakings. It is assessed that regarding esteem, MSME segment represents about 45% of the assembling yield and around 40% of the all-out fare of the nation.

1.1.9. The concept of self-efficacy belief and its role in workplace

As indicated by social-subjective scholar (Bandura, 1997; 2000a) individual viability conviction is the center establishment of human organization. Individuals vary in convictions about their competency and achievement in various space of their life. Bandura (1997) called these comprehensions self-adequacy, which are convictions in one's own capacities to sort out and execute the game-plan required to create the given fulfillments.

Self-adequacy conviction assumes an essential job in work setting. Individuals spend a significant piece of their lives in word related exercises. Seen self-adequacy assumes a key job in what individuals pick as their labor of love, the amazing way well they set themselves up for their picked interests, and the achievement they accomplish in their ordinary work. In depicting the job of apparent self-adequacy in human improvement when all is said in done, Bandura (2004) recommended that transformational social change offer supremacy to individual and aggregate organization in this electronic time. Among the instrument of conviction framework is the establishment of human organization. Except if individuals accept they can deliver wanted results and thwart undesired ones by their activities, they have minimal impetus to act or to continue on despite troubles. Whatever different components fill in as aides and inspirations, they are established in the center conviction that one has the ability to deliver changes by one's activities. The unmistakable trait of individuals who make progress in testing interests is an unwavering feeling of viability and a firm confidence in the value they are doing. Flexible viability gives the required backbone. The individuals who are fruitful, inventive, non on edge, non-miserable and relentless social reformers take a hopeful perspective on their adequacy to impact occasions that influence their lives (Bandura, 1997; Mc Elroy, 2002). According to Bandura (1997), efficacy beliefs regulate human functioning through four major processes: cognitive, motivational, emotional, and choice processes. They affect whether individuals think pessimistically or optimistically, in self-enhancing or self-debilitating ways. How well they motivate themselves and persevere in the face of difficulties. Even the quality of their emotional well-being and their vulnerability to stress and depression are also affected by efficacy beliefs.

Sources of self-efficacy

In the writing of self-efficacy (for example Bandura, 1997 and 2000a; McElroy, 2002) four wellsprings of adequacy conviction were examined. They are: enactive mastery, vicarious experience, verbal/social influence, and physiological and full of feeling states.

A. **Enactive mastery**

The main, wellspring of viability, enactive authority, alludes to information and expertise increased through understanding and diligence. All together for self-efficacy to be increased, a few disappointments must be experienced. In the event that achievement comes too effectively, the individual is probably going to feel to a lesser degree a feeling of achievement and sentiments of mastery are probably going to be decreased. At the point when little disappointments are experienced, the individual has the chance to make change in accordance with moves made and practice better command over what is occurring. Along these lines, a supported exertion prompts a more noteworthy feeling of self-adequacy. Dynamic mastery has been appeared to upgrade sentiment of self-adequacy and improve diagnostic thinking, objective setting, and execution. Regardless of whether achievement or disappointment happens is less significant than how the individual sees the essentialness of the occasion and the person's general ability. Enactive mastery has been seen as the most powerful wellspring of self-viability, prompting more grounded and increasingly summed up sentiments of self-adequacy which are depicted underneath.

B. **Vicarious experience**

Vicarious experience alludes to the experience of others utilized as a model and as a level of examination about what aptitudes are important to finish an undertaking. This may include watching another person who is capable at an assignment and checking whether one has the potential and determination to achieve the equivalent or a more significant level of ability. Numerous elements are related with how significant vicarious experience is as a wellspring of self-viability, including the degree of aptitude at the time that demonstrating is watched and similitudes between the individual and the individual who is filling in as the model. The individuals who are like the eyewitness with respect to age, ethnicity and instructive and financial level frequently fill in as the best models and are bound to expand the onlooker's sentiments of self-adequacy. It has additionally been indicated that watching a person who must adapt to challenges preceding encountering achievement viable in expanding self-adequacy than watching a person who can ace the action with little battle.

C. **Verbal or social persuasion**

Verbal or social influence serves to strengthen sentiment of adequacy when confronting the minor disappointments referenced previously. Albeit social influence isn't simply the most vital strategy where adequacy is fortified, it makes it simpler for individual to keep up constancy and confidence in them encountering sentiments of uncertainty. For social influence to be compelling, it should originate from somebody who the individual feels is a dependable wellspring of criticism.

D. **Physiological and affective states**

An individual's physical response to troublesome circumstances can impact how arranged that individual feels to successfully deal with the circumstance. On the off chance that an individual feels overpowering sentiment of stress, the person in question is probably going to question their capacity to do the assignment. It is comprehended that when past occasions are recalled, the emotions related with those occasions are frequently recollected and even re-experienced too. This can directly affect whether an individual can keep up sentiment of inspiration and steadiness even with deterrents and disappointment. Thusly, adjusting a person's impression of physical response to troublesome circumstances, for example, emotions identified with pressure, dread, or humiliation, can incredibly influence sentiments of self-viability.

Self-adequacy has any kind of effect in how individuals feel, think, and act. Individuals with high self-viability decide to perform all the more testing assignments. They set themselves more significant standards and stick to them. Activities are pre-molded in thought, and once a move has been made, profoundly self-effectual individuals contribute more exertion and endure longer than those low in self-viability. At the point when difficulties happen, they recoup all the more rapidly and stay focused on their objectives. High self-viability likewise enables individuals to choose testing settings and investigate their condition or make new ones. Therefore, it exhibits a faith in one's ability in managing a wide range of requests. This suggests an interior stable attribution of fruitful activity and a planned view. As per different writing (e.g., Bandura, 1997,

Luszczynska, Gutie'rrez-Dona and Schwarzer, 2005) this trademark make it a one of a kind hypothetical develop not quite the same as related ones, for example, confidence, locus of control, or self-idea of capacity. Confidence has an enthusiastic undertone. Locus of control alludes to an attribution of obligation regarding results (inside organization versus outer causation), and self-idea of capacity relates to a judgment of one's capability without reference to any consequent activity. Just self-adequacy is of a forthcoming and employable nature, which outfits this build with extra illustrative and prescient power in an assortment of research applications (Luszczynska et al, 2005).

Dimensions of self-efficacy belief and entrepreneurial success

As examined before, perceived self-efficacy can be described chiefly as being capability based, imminent, and activity related, instead of comparative develops that offer just piece of this depiction (Bandura, 1992, and Luszczynska et al., 2005). As per a few examinations (Jex and Gudanowski, 1992; Schultz and Schultz, 2002; Goddard et al., 2004) self-viability conviction has different perspectives, for example, general self-adequacy, aggregate self-adequacy, and circumstance/task explicit efficacies, for example, educator self-adequacy conviction, pioneering self-adequacy conviction and expert adequacy conviction. As the examination focused on miniaturized scale and little business visionaries, writing relates to enterprising self-adequacy conviction and aggregate viability conviction was investigated here.

Entrepreneurial self-efficacy and entrepreneurial success

As examined before self-viability, in association with work is identified with how a lot of undertaking exertion exhausted and to what extent that exertion will be supported in spite of difficulties. From social learning hypothesis it tends to be noticed that people who see themselves as exceptionally effectual enact adequate exertion that, if professional, produces adequate results, while the individuals who see low self-viability are probably going to stop their endeavors rashly and bomb on the undertaking. Studies directed by Goddard et al. (2004), stajkovic and Lutansa, (1998) showed the positive connection between self-adequacy and distinctive inspirational and conduct results in clinical, instructive and authoritative setting. In particular, in hierarchical setting concerning connection between self-adequacy and execution, drawing on an audit of different writing stajkovic and Lutansa (1998) demonstrated relationship of self-viability with various business related execution estimates, for example, flexibility to cutting edge innovation, adapting to vocation related occasions, administrative thought age, administrative execution, aptitude obtaining, and newcomers change in accordance with authoritative setting.

In zone of work which is enterprising in nature, there are additionally confirms for criticalness of self-adequacy. By its very nature, the advancement of new business adventures and the restoration of set up ones depend vigorously on creativity and enterprise. Such interests are strewn with hindrances and vulnerabilities.

Transforming dreams into truths is a laborious procedure with dubious results. Business, in this manner, may require a vigorous viability to support through the anxieties and demoralization innate in imaginative interests.

Self-viability identified with the errand of enterprise is pioneering self-adequacy at first present by Chen et al. (1998). As indicated by the scientists, enterprising self-viability alludes to the quality of an individual's conviction that the individual is able to do effectively playing out the different jobs and assignments of business enterprise. The enterprising self-adequacy proposed by these specialists comprises of five elements; viz., advertising, development, the board, hazard taking and money related control. The analysts directed two examinations, one on understudies the other on independent company administrators. Discoveries got from these investigations explained that the all-out innovative self-adequacy conviction score separated enterprise understudies from non-business understudies; pioneering self-viability was decidedly identified with the expectation to arrangement one's very own business, and furthermore enterprise understudies to have higher self-viability in showcasing, the executives and monetary control than non-enterprise understudies. Moreover, it was additionally seen that business authors had higher self-adequacy in advancement and hazard taking than did non originators. Subsequently, consequences of the examination exhibit the capability of pioneering self-viability as an unmistakable trait of business people.

Following the presentation of the development of pioneering self-adequacy conviction numerous studies (Hhallak, 2008; Lindsay et al., 2006; Pushkarskaya and Usher, 2010; Zhao et al., 2005) analyzed its associations with enterprise especially innovative aim and numerous innovative results including pioneering execution. In view of survey of different examinations, Hallak (2008) for example, recommended the positive relations of innovative self-viability with enterprising execution. As per

Hallak's (2008) survey, innovative self-adequacy influences enterprising execution from numerous points of view. Initially, the more noteworthy the degree of self-viability of the business visionary, the more prominent the probability that the business drove by the business visionary embraces an innovative direction, since business with an enterprising direction has been appeared to perform superior to other non-pioneering business, second, pioneering self-adequacy influences execution in that it impacts the business visionary's advantage, inspirations and persistence. Third, innovative self-adequacy is likewise connected with objective setting those with higher pioneering self-viability more significant standards for themselves and their business and they will likewise be increasingly persevering in their endeavors to attempt to arrive at these objectives. Forward, pioneering self-viability likewise fortifies exertion, which thusly reinforces execution, and can likewise impact the adequacy with which business visionaries deal with their business. Fifth, pioneering self-viability additionally influences the person's capacity to manage dangers and vulnerabilities, which are common attributes of business enterprise.

1.1.10. DEFINING QUALITY OF LIFE

The expression "personal satisfaction" covers yet isn't synonymous with various terms, including "prosperity," "social pointers," and "lifestyle" among others (Andrews, 1980). Numerous examiners around there have embraced the expression "level of prosperity" as one that appears to express the personal satisfaction idea most briefly. In any case, the definition that will be alluded to all through this report is to some degree more extensive than the one proposed by Rice (1984): The personal satisfaction is how much the experience of a person's life fulfills that person's needs and needs (both physical and mental).

A significant part of the discussion about how personal satisfaction ought to be characterized has based on abstract versus target draws near. Rice further characterizes target personal satisfaction (OQL) as how much determined ways of life are met by the equitably undeniable conditions, exercises, and action outcomes of a person's life, and abstract personal satisfaction (SQL) as a lot of full of feeling convictions coordinated toward one's life.

Hence, characteristic in the goal/emotional discussion is the topic of who ought to decide how well the person's needs and needs have been fulfilled. The target approach relies on the judgment of a tip top who have determined models that they accept will fulfill human needs,

The emotional methodology enables people to characterize for themselves the nature of their lives and perceives the probability of a large number of various directions (Blishen and Atkinson, 1980). In general, legislative offices have favored target draws near while overview associations with scholarly affiliations ordinarily have embraced emotional methodologies. The ideas of bliss and fulfillment establish a basic piece of life quality. At the point when individuals get more joyful, they become progressively happy with their lives, employments, and fulfillments.

1.1.11. Entrepreneurial Well-being

Most work analyzing the connection among business enterprise and prosperity has received one of two draws near—either depending on general proportions of prosperity, (for example, life fulfilment and positive effect) or concentrating on setting explicit develops of business-and business related fulfilment (e.g., Benz and Frey, 2008; Block and Koellinger, 2009; Bradley and Roberts, 2004; Cooper and Artz, 1995). While both these arrangement of measures pass on significant data about the prosperity of venturesome people, it is dicey that they speak to the by and large prosperity that people get from commitment in innovative exercises. Specifically, the estimation and conceptualization of innovative prosperity as an unmistakable encounter of prosperity has gotten little consideration up until now, in spite of many years of research on prosperity throughout everyday life and work. Truth be told, the brain science and authoritative work writing consider setting explicit proportions of prosperity in non-work settings as satisfactory and separate proportions of prosperity (Warr, 1990; Cotton and Hart, 2003; Page and Vella-Brodrick, 2009). By concentrating either on one's general life appraisal or on an element of the business or the work itself, prior measures don't catch the emotional and center general understanding of prosperity in enterprise. For instance, business people detailing general constructive life fulfillment and fulfillment with business execution may likewise express lower joy and satisfaction with life as a business person, proposing a setting explicit nature of the build (George, 1980). An expansive and more straightforward proportion of prosperity in business enterprise is probably going to more readily reflect singular encounters of prosperity in this area (Shir, 2015). Thusly, setting explicit conceptualizations and proportions of abstract prosperity in business enterprise ought to give a progressively complete estimation of the emotional prizes experienced by business people and extend hypothetical and experimental research skylines. In view of these general improvements, we characterize innovative prosperity as "the experience of fulfillment, constructive effect, rare contrary effect, and mental working in connection to creating, beginning, developing, and running a pioneering adventure." Psychological working incorporates self-acknowledgment, self-awareness, reason (which means), emotional well-being, dominance, self-rule, and positive relations, among others. We offer this as a beginning stage for future work hypothesizing and estimating business visionaries' emotional encounters and related target individual and ecological settings that influence prosperity while creating, beginning, developing, and running a pioneering adventure.

1.2. Research in context

So as to test the connection between social business and personal satisfaction or abstract prosperity, optional information from the studies that speak to rankings of countries, utilizing criteria of social enterprise and personal satisfaction or emotional prosperity, have been investigated. This is accessible just from a concentrate the information on 47 chose nations from studies, directed in 2009 through 2011. Note that the information on social business enterprise on which this paper has been based sole overview displayed by Bosma, Levie and Global Entrepreneurship Research Association (2010).

Business enterprise is a helpful budgetary advancement apparatus in troublesome monetary occasions, and female business visionaries are frequently an undiscovered and underestimated asset with the possibility to support financial achievement (Allen et al., 2007). It has been placed that when the prosperity of any burdened gathering of individuals is advanced, it will in the long run create neighborhood networks and economies (Birley, 1989; Gray and Collins-Williams, 2006). Through business enterprise, it is conceivable to figure out how to coordinate and enable minority and underestimated gatherings, making upward versatility and shortening work advertise segregation. Business enterprise at that point gives significant choices when other monetary open doors are not accessible (Fairlie, 2004; Minniti and Arenius, 2003; Rochin et al., 1998; Verdaguerand Vallas, 2008; Zhou, 2004).

Internationally, the quantity of ladies entrepreneurs is step by step expanding, and it has been assessed that organizations which are run and claimed by ladies represent somewhere in the range of 25% and 33% all things considered. It is proposed by Tominc and Rebernik (2003: 781) that separated from producing a significant measure of GOP, ladies are likewise impacting how the business network, the general population, authorities and the media see and reacts to them. A significant point to be noted here is that female business people are not taken as a very enormous gathering in business segment. They are treated as a shifted and unpredictable gathering with wide-running foundations, circumstances and perspectives. The consequence of this is the investigation of ladies and enterprise is developing (McKay, 2001).

As per Aldrich (1989), female business people face challenges due to social structures (work environment, family and sorted out public activity). He calls attention to that ladies' business execution is adversely affected by word related isolation and underrepresentation in upper-level administration positions (Ibid). He additionally expresses that the desires society holds about family jobs may restrict ladies' support in business to certain modern parts and furthermore influence the idea of inspirations and objectives as to their endeavors (Ibid).

Sociological scholars contend that social structures (the work environment, the family and sorted out public activity) make issues for ladies, preventing them from getting enterprising openings and affecting their presentation (Aldrich, 1989). Baughn et al. (2006) have talked about the way that various nations have various standards with respect to sex and these notably affect specific perspectives on female business; they note that talks likewise influence general thinking, and they express that enterprise is typically portrayed as a normally male wonder in a large portion of the pioneering talk (Bruni et al., 2004; Godwin et al., 2006; Mattis, 2004). Dispositions towards enterprise are a piece of the business condition and these additionally have enormous criticalness for female business people (Baeva, 2004). There are social perspectives and suppositions which demoralize ladies business people; these elements hinder enterprise (Maas and Herrington, 2006: 41). It is called attention to by Lerner et al. (1997) that the degree to which female business visionaries experience auxiliary obstructions contrarily impacts the presentation of their endeavors.

A typical view today is that the advancement of society is emphatically dependent on sex balance. In any case, Landes (2003) has seen that sexual orientation imbalances stay inactive around the world. Female business people face difficulties of different sorts, which incorporate "level of instruction", "between job clashes exuding from more noteworthy child rearing duties", "Absence of monetary support" and "socio-social constraints" (Ghosh and Cheruvalath, 2007: 150). It is a typical perception that the two people experience individual issues, however ladies face a lot a greater number of troubles than men. A few creators (Roomi and Parriot, 2008; Goheer, 2002; Kuratko and Welsch, 1994; Hisrich and Oztirk, 1999; Breen et al., 1995; Cannon, 1991; Hisrich and Peters, 1989; Watson, 2003; Fay and Williams, 1993) point out that when female business people attempt to get an advance toward the beginning up arrange or to grow their organizations they face a great deal of issues. As ladies need to confront such a significant number of issues so as to acquire money related guide they as a rule restrain themselves to low-capital concentrated exercises (Bruni et al., 2004).

Variables like word related isolation and conventional family jobs can limit a lady's decision of business area as well as the objectives she sets for her endeavor (Aldrich 1989).

The basic obstructions that ladies can confront majorly affect the exhibition of their endeavors. The nation wherein a lady lives additionally identifies with the troubles she is probably going to confront. In certain nations, ladies are generally less expected to perform pioneering jobs (Sekarun and Leong, 1992).

Another obstacle looked by ladies business people is an absence of business-related information and access to systems administration and bolster components (Allen and Truman, 1993). Open strategy activities to furnish ladies with simple access to data; aptitude improvement and financing (OECD, 1993; Allen and Truman, 1993) are in progress in many creating nations.

Notwithstanding, in nations like the US and Canada the circumstance is unique and ladies have simple access to preparing, interpersonal interaction and data sources (OECD, 1993; Brush, 1992).

Bowen and Hisrich, (1986), looked at and assessed different research thinks about done on business enterprise including ladies business. It rundowns different investigations along these lines that female business visionaries are moderately knowledgeable when all is said in done yet maybe not in the executives abilities, high in inner locus of control, progressively manly, or instrumental than other ladies in their qualities prone to have had enterprising dads, generally liable to have posts conceived or just youngsters, far-fetched to begin business in customarily male ruled ventures and encountering a need of extra administrative preparing.

Cohoon, Wadhwa and Mitchell, (2010), present an itemized investigation of men and ladies business person's inspirations, foundation and encounters. The investigation depends on the information gathered from fruitful ladies business people. Out of them 59% had established at least two organizations. The examination recognizes top five money related and mental variables propelling ladies to become business visionaries.

These are want to construct the riches, the desire to underwrite claim business thoughts they had, the intrigue of start-up culture, a long standing want to possess their own organization and working with another person didn't bid them. The difficulties are more related with business instead of sexual orientation. In any case, the examination closed with the prerequisite of further examination like why ladies are such a great amount of worried about securing scholarly capital than their partner.

Coaching is imperative to ladies, which gives consolation and budgetary backing of colleagues, encounters and very much created proficient system. Ladies organize report on Women in Business and in Decision Making center around ladies business visionaries, about their issues in beginning and maintaining the business, family back ground, training, size of specialty unit. Some intriguing certainties which turned out from this report are less taught ladies business visionaries are occupied with miniaturized scale undertakings, have spouse and kids however have no assistance at home.

The majority of the ladies set up ventures before the age of 35, in the wake of increasing some understanding as a worker elsewhere. The inspirational components were want for control and opportunity to accept their very own choice just as acquiring attractive measure of cash. Commitment of over 48 hours in seven days with the family backing to their ventures gave them a feeling of self-assurance. Be that as it may, to keep up balance between family and work life is a significant test before ladies business people particularly for the individuals who have kids and working spouse.

Darrene, Harpel and Mayer, (2008) played out an investigation on finding the connection between components of human capital and independent work among ladies. The investigation demonstrated that independently employed ladies contrast on most human capital variable when contrasted with the compensation and blue collar ladies. The investigation likewise uncovered the way that the instruction accomplishment level is quicker for independently employed ladies than that for other working ladies. The level of inhabitance of administrative occupation is seen as similarly higher if there should arise an occurrence of independently employed ladies when contrasted with other working ladies.

This investigation additionally shed light on comparability and uniqueness of circumstances for independently employed men and independently employed ladies. Independently employed people contrast little in training, experience and readiness. Be that as it may, the principle distinction lies in word related and industry experience. The level of populace holding the executives occupation is lower for independently employed ladies when contrasted with independently employed men. Additionally the cooperation levels of independently employed ladies are seen as not exactly of independently employed men in businesses like correspondence, transportation, discount exchange, assembling and development. The examination depends on information from the Current Population Survey (CPS) Annual Social and Economic Supplement (ASEC) from 1994 to 2006.

Singh, 2008, distinguishes the reasons and affecting variables behind passage of ladies in business enterprise. He clarified the attributes of their organizations in Indian setting and furthermore impediments and difficulties. He referenced the impediments in the development of ladies business enterprise are for the most part absence of communication with effective business people, social un-acknowledgment as ladies business visionaries, family obligation, sexual orientation segregation, missing system, low need given by financiers to give credit to ladies business people. He recommended the medicinal estimates like advancing smaller scale endeavors, opening institutional edge work, anticipating and dismantling to develop and bolster the victors and so forth. The investigation advocates for guaranteeing collaboration among ladies related service, monetary service and social and welfare advancement service of the Government of India.

Tambunan, (2009), made an investigation on late improvements of ladies business visionaries in Asian creating nations. The investigation concentrated fundamentally on ladies business people in little and medium ventures dependent on information examination and audit of ongoing key writing. This examination found that in Asian creating nations SMEs are increasing overpowering significance; over 95% of all organizations in all areas overall per nation. The examination likewise delineated the way that portrayal of ladies business people in this area is moderately low because of elements like low degree of training, absence of capital and social or strict limitations. In any case, the examination uncovered that the greater part of the ladies business people in SMEs are from the class of constrained business visionaries looking for better family livelihoods.

1.3. Need for the study:

India has been a place that is known for business visionaries. Business has been considered as one of the basic components deciding the development of industry in any nation. The historical backdrop of monetary improvement of all nations in the case of creating or created, has confirm the way that business visionaries have made a huge commitment in this regard. The nature and degree of such commitment shifts from society to society, and nation to nation; contingent on the modern atmosphere, material sources and the obligation of political framework (Yadav, 1999). In another investigation (Balu,1992) cites that business enterprise advancement is fundamental for expanding the generation and profitability in the essential, optional and tertiary parts and saddling and using the material and HR, taking care of the issue of joblessness and underemployment affecting fair circulation of salary and riches. This thus builds Gross National Product (GNP) and per capita pay and improving the personal satisfaction. The commitment of little business visionaries has been constantly expanding since 1950. It was additionally been seen that the quantity of prepared business visionaries was quickly expanding in each area of India. With globalization and information based society spreading like out of control fire on the planet today, the acknowledgment of ladies' urgent job in human advancement has been picking up acknowledgment. Ladies today face numerous difficulties and will confront more current ones in future. They will presently need to confront increasingly stringent types of rivalry. They should clean their current aptitude of riches creation and time the executives to manage the difficulties of 21st century. They should commit increasingly more time to get new expertise and information, which presently maintain the wheels of business and industry on the planet. Thus, the researcher expected to discover the self-efficacy and quality of life among women entrepreneurs.

1.4. Objectives of the study

The main objectives of the present study are to examine self-efficacy and quality of life as a factor in influencing women entrepreneurs. Specifically, the current study deals with:

- To Identify factors influencing women entrepreneurs
- To explore the extent of Self efficacy among women entrepreneurs of Andhra Pradesh.
- To study the extent of Quality of Life among women entrepreneurs of Andhra Pradesh.

- To examine the differences in the Self efficacy among women entrepreneurs based on demographic variables such as age, marital status, education, type of industries, and type of business and years of establishment among entrepreneurs.

- To outline the differences in the Quality of life among women entrepreneurs based on demographic variables such as Age, Marital Status, Education, Type of Industries, Type of Business and Years of established among entrepreneurs.

- To see the relationship between Self efficacy and Quality of life among women entrepreneurs.

1.5. Hypotheses

- There will be a significant difference in self-efficacy among women entrepreneurs based on demographic variables such as age, marital status, education, type of industries, type of business and years of established.

- There will be a significant difference between demographical variables such as Age, Marital Status, Education, Type of Industries, Type of Business and modify in the same way as #1. Years of established with Quality of life among entrepreneurs.

- There will be positive relationship between Self efficacy and Quality of life among entrepreneurs.

1.6. Significance of Research

The current study will provide a set of critical success factors and critical failure factors model for women entrepreneurs in Andhra Pradesh. The study also highlights the importance self-efficacy and quality of life as an influencing factors that essential to achieve women entrepreneur success, as well as critical failure factors in order to avoid women entrepreneur failure. The results can be useful in optimizing the local women entrepreneurial performance by presenting both success and failure factors that significantly influence the business operating performance.

Chapter two

Review of related literature

2.1. An overview to entrepreneurship

As globalization reshapes the worldwide monetary scene and mechanical change makes more noteworthy vulnerability on the planet economy, the dynamism of business enterprise is accepted to have the option to meet the new financial, social and natural difficulties. Governments progressively believe business enterprise and advancement to be the foundations of a focused national economy, and in many nations business enterprise arrangements are in actuality firmly associated with development approaches, with which they share numerous attributes and difficulties. The dynamic procedure of new firm creation presents and scatters inventive items, forms and hierarchical structures all through the economy. Business enterprise destinations and strategies by the by vary extensively among nations, attributable to various approach needs and different points of view on what is implied by business. On the side of this Schumpeter (2005) expressed,

In certain nations, business enterprise is connected to territorial advancement programs and the production of new firms is animated to support work and yield in discouraged districts. In others, business enterprise is a key component of procedures intended to encourage the investment of certain objective gatherings, for example, ladies or minorities, in the economy. A few nations just look to expand firm creation in that capacity, while others set out to help high-development firms. While numerous nations are attempting genuine endeavors to help enterprise, results seem to differ. Nations need to comprehend the determinants of and deterrents to business enterprise, and they have to break down the viability of various arrangement draws near (p.13)

The absence of universally practically identical exact proof has anyway compelled our comprehension of enterprise and numerous inquiries stay unanswered. At last approach causing must to be guided, beyond what many would consider possible, by proof and actualities.

2.2. Meaning and definitions of entrepreneurship

There is no agreement among creators with respect to the meanings of Entrepreneurship. Various creators attempted to characterize it in various habits. This doesn't mean anyway that there are no basic components among creators. A portion of the definitions are given underneath.

As per Ponstadt (1998): Entrepreneurship is the dynamic procedure of making steady riches. This riches is made by people who accept the significant dangers as far as value, time or potentially vocation responsibilities of giving qualities to some item or administration. The item or administration may/may not be new or interesting however esteem must be implanted by the business visionary by verifying and designating the essential abilities and assets (p.9)

Moreover, Timmons (1989) characterized it so that: Entrepreneurship is the way toward making and building something of significant worth from for all intents and purposes nothing. That is, it is the way toward making or taking advantage of a lucky break and seeking after it paying little heed to the assets right now controlled. It includes the definition, creation and conveyance of qualities and advantages to people, gatherings, associations and society. Enterprise is once in a while a make easy money recommendation (not present moment); rather it is one of building long haul esteem and solid income streams (p.29)

Moreover, Hisrich (2005 :) characterized business as pursues: Entrepreneurship is the way toward making something new with esteem by giving the essential time and exertion, expecting the going with money related, clairvoyant, and social dangers, and accepting the subsequent prizes of fiscal and individual fulfillment and freedom (p.2)

From the definitions given above, it is conceivable to presume that in practically the entirety of the meanings of business enterprise, there is understanding that we are discussing a sort of conduct that incorporates: (1) activity taking, (2) the arranging and revamping of social and monetary systems to turn assets and circumstances to down to earth account, (3) the acknowledgment of hazard or disappointment.

2.3. The benefits of entrepreneurship

It is liberally evident that business enterprise is significant for financial development, efficiency, advancement and work, and numerous nations have made business unequivocal approach need. Pioneering exercises have been perceived as a significant component in hierarchical and monetary advancement, execution and riches creation. As indicated by World Bank (2007), Fox (2001) and Hisrich (2005) enterprise has the accompanying advantages.

1. Business people work for themselves. They settle on the choices. They pick whom to work with and what work they will do. They choose what hours to work, just as what to pay and whether to take get-aways.
2. Business offers a more noteworthy probability of accomplishing critical money related prizes than working for another person.

3. It gives the capacity to be engaged with the absolute activity of the business, from idea to plan and creation, from deals to business tasks and client reaction.

4. It offers the notoriety of being the individual in control.

5. It offers an individual the chance to fabricate value, which can be kept, sold, or gave to the people to come.

6. Enterprise makes an open door for an individual to make a commitment. Most new business people help the neighborhood economy. A couple — through their advancements — add to society.

7. It is an impetus for financial change and development .Entrepreneurship increment per capita yield and pay .By doing so it includes starting and establishing change in the structure of business and society. Subsequently business enterprise contribute a ton in expanding nations yield and efficiency

8. Business energizes development and inventiveness. It grows new items or administration for the market to satisfy human needs. It likewise animates speculation enthusiasm for the new pursuits being made. Business enterprise through its procedure of advancement makes new speculation of new pursuits .More adventures being made, new openings will be created, in this way diminish the joblessness rate. That will makes and advances riches conveyance as clarified above, entrepreneurism helps the economy by making riches for some, people looking for business openings. Despite the fact that this isn't the main explanation people seek after business visionary exercises, it assumes a significant job in our economy. Both another business and the riches the proprietor can acquire will help support the economy by giving new items just as the spending influence made for the business visionary.

9. Without business people, our economy would not profit by the lift they give from included business and thoughts. Moreover, beginning a business can be fulfilling. Business people work for themselves.

10. They can have more authority over their working hours and conditions than they would have on the off chance that they worked for another person. In the event that they can't get a new line of work they need, they can start a new business to make one. For instance, they may have another thought regarding a specific item or administration. On the off chance that they accept that others would be keen on it, they can start a new business for themselves. They may make a benefit, which is the cash left over in the wake of covering their tabs, from being innovative and doing what they appreciate.

2.4. Nature of women entrepreneurs

There is no agreement among scientists as to the distinctions in the qualities of male and female business visionaries. A few gatherings of analysts concur that there are no distinctions. Be that as it may, some others state contrasts. For instance Green and Cohen (1995) expressed, "A business visionary is a business person is a business person," and it ought not to make any difference what size, shape, shading, or sex the business visionary may be. Provided that this is true, great research on business visionaries ought to produce hypothesis appropriate to all. While investigate shows likenesses in the individual socioeconomics of people business people, there are contrasts in business and industry decisions, financing systems, development examples, and administration structures of female drove adventures (p.106)

These distinctions give convincing motivations to think about female business – taking a gander at ladies originators, their endeavors, and their pioneering practices as a one of a kind subset of enterprise. Similarly as we have discovered that clinical preliminaries directed on an all-male populace don't really give precise data about the determination or treatment of female patients, we see that academic research concentrated distinctly on male enterprising endeavors leaves numerous inquiries unanswered for their female partners. Some contend that it is critical to take a gander at female business people who, however they share numerous attributes with their male partners, are one of a kind in numerous perspectives.

Noticeable contrasts in their ventures reflect basic contrasts in their inspirations and objectives, arrangement, association, vital direction, and access to assets.

Birley (1987) worried on the distinctions even in their experience and individual qualities. He saw the female business visionaries as the main conceived; from a center or privileged family; the little girl of an independently employed dad; taught to degree level; wedded with kids; forty to forty-five at fire up; and with important experience

In their craving in beginning new organizations, specialists distinguished various explanations behind ladies to become business visionaries. South Africa Entrepreneurs Network (2005) as cited in: *http://www.dti.gov.za/sawen/SAWENreport2.pdf* called attention to that difficulties/attractions of business; self-assurance/self-rule; family concerns – adjusting profession and family; absence of professional success/separation; and authoritative elements control/governmental issues are accounted for as fundamental initiators to become business visionaries for ladies. The report likewise added the craving to make a social commitment and helping other people has been seen as a key factor in ladies deciding to become entrepreneurs.

2.5. Factors relating to women entrepreneurs

Different investigate endeavors were attempted to distinguish factors affecting the presentation of ladies business visionaries as confirm from the writing and earlier studies, these elements being examined in a divided manner and led among the created countries. It is of foremost significance for the ladies business visionaries to grasp these elements as they bear considerable effect on their business execution, particularly when they contend in this difficult, globalized business field.

It is a general faith in numerous societies that the job of ladies is to fabricate and keeps up the unattractive issues like errand of getting water, cooking and raising kids. Since the turn of the century, the status of ladies in India has been changing because of developing industrialization, globalization, and social enactment. With the spread of training and mindfulness, ladies have moved from kitchen to more significant level of expert action.

Enterprise has been a male-overwhelmed marvel from the early age, yet time has changed the circumstance and brought ladies as the present generally vital and moving business visionaries. In practically all the created nations on the planet ladies and placing their means at standard with the men in field of business. The job of Women business visionary in financial improvement is unavoidable. Presently a-days ladies enter in chosen callings as well as in callings like exchange, industry and designing.

Ladies are additionally ready to take up business and add to the country's development. Their job is additionally being perceived and steps are being taken to advance ladies business. Ladies business must be formed appropriately with enterprising attributes and aptitudes to meet the adjustments in patterns, challenges worldwide markets and furthermore be equipped enough to continue and make progress toward greatness in the innovative field.

The accompanying segment talks about the definitions and variables affecting execution of ladies business people dependent on the audit of writing that have collected great hypothetical and reasonable help. At the point when appropriate presentation, training and information are bestowed to them, Indian ladies will demonstrate themselves to be exceptionally potential gainful power for the advancement of the country. The monetary, social, strict, social, and mental components influence start and accomplishment of ladies business people Habib, Roni, and Haque (2005). The reasons and inspirations for beginning business or monetary exercises by the country ladies are colossal. The significant reasons are gaining cash or alluring wellspring of pay, getting a charge out of better life, accessibility of advances, ideal government arrangement, impact of examples of overcoming adversity, individual fulfillment, want to use claim expertise and gifts, horrible present workplace, independent work and work of others, confirmation of vocation and family security, satisfaction of innovative inclination of the borrowers' involvement with privately-run company, self-assurance, non-capacity to secure appropriate position or work, consolation and exhortation of the relatives, financial need, etc. Ladies' purposes behind beginning business are not in every case frequently determined by positive factors yet in addition because of negative conditions, for example, low family income, absence of work openings, and disappointment with a present place of employment or the requirement for adaptable work Robinson (2001).

2.5.1. Socio-Family Factors:

Social Factors

These are things that influence way of life, for example, religion, family or riches. These can change after some time. The term social elements allude to the realities and encounters that impact or control a person's character, demeanors and way of life. These components help an individual live well in congruity with others in the general public.

A social factor is a viewpoint in life that effects and impacts the human conduct in the general public. It manages that everybody in the general public ought to carry on in a steady way and ought to comply with every one of the guidelines of the general public.

Social factors will be factors that affect or direct individuals' ways of life in a given society. Model include: religion, ethnicity, family, monetary status and instruction. These components are available in a multi-social society. Social factors are things in our general public which influence or direct our way of life. A few models are religion, family, training, territory and financial status.

Family Factors

Certain life circumstances, for example, single child rearing, aggressive behavior at home and other unpleasant occasions, can add to the probability of abuse, especially when guardians are separated socially or need adequate enthusiastic or monetary help.

Shim and Eestlick (1993) found that ladies have less work understanding and their organizations were more youthful than men. Subsequently, they absence of systems or contact, socialization practices and family jobs.Masudet al. (1999) in a concentrate on small scale venture through 319 ladies in Peninsular Malaysia found that ladies picked up information through their activities in overseeing and controlling gainful assets, expertise, and experience, and an expansion in their capacity to source important data and take care of issues that prepare them to become business visionaries and setting the business effectively.

From the natural point of view, family impact, especially parental impact has been found as the predecessor of private company vocation intrigue.

Relatives, particularly guardians assume a key job in setting up the attractive quality and validity of pioneering activity for people. Scherer et al. (1989) found that the nearness of a parent innovative good example was related with a person's business execution. People with a parent pioneering good example were seen to be superior workers and were altogether not the same as people without innovative good examples, who were seen to be low entertainers. Most of effective ladies business visionaries recognized one parent as being progressively compelling, that is, numerous fruitful ladies distinguish emphatically with their dads Henning and Jardim (1978) and Belcourt et al's. (1991) study announced that 33 percent of Canadian ladies business people studied expressed their dads were business visionaries. This is consistent as parent-youngster relationship advances accomplishment endeavoring and freedom. Stein& Bailey, (1973).Female work power cooperation likewise is by all accounts identified with the frame of mind of the family towards ladies. Aminah (1998), for example, in an investigation of chose effective profession ladies in Malaysia, uncovered that changing mentalities of guardians and spouses towards a progressively positive pattern were seen to be identified with higher instructive accomplishment of ladies which thusly could impact ladies' cooperation in the work power by setting up their own organizations.

In accordance with the social learning hypothesis, the guardians must be urged to rouse their youngsters, especially girls to wander into business enterprise. On the off chance that the facts confirm that enterprising guardians impact their little girls to become business people, at that point these endeavors by the administration and colleges won't get most extreme outcomes if most of guardians are not business people. By and by, if this idea remains constant, the present ladies age who adventure into enterprise will make a bigger pool of ladies business visionaries of the people to come. Ladies and men business visionaries will in general perform in an unexpected way. In addition, their life partners assume significant jobs in urging their innovative spouses to join and partake in the exercises of these affiliations.

How a general public contemplates business may impact the pool of potential business visionaries. The draw among family and work and the various other social jobs that ladies play can be found in how job strife is experienced–paying little respect to family structure or time spent at work. This contention was seen as increasingly predominant in proprietors with lower confidence or self-esteem. Stoner, Hartman, and Arora (1990): One examination found the connection between time responsibility to work and time promise to family intervened the impact of job requests. Parasuraman, Purohit,

Godshalk & Beutell (1996): As a feature of the thought of these jobs, the commitment of both expressive and instrumental help from the life partners was regularly given. Greene (1993): In an investigation of 48 participants at a business enterprise instruction program, Birley et al. (1987) found that men got support from their mates in their business undertakings more frequently than did ladies. Biggart's (1988): Charismatic Capitalism incorporates numerous frequencies of ladies associated with direct selling exercises, who were required to work around their companions, as opposed to getting support from them. For ladies business visionaries, parenthood or family inserting will legitimately impact how the innovative procedure unfurls. Family job will impact data systems used to recognize the market opportunity.

Henceforth, ladies with high duty to family will be less inclined to cooperate in showcase/monetary/industry systems, perhaps influencing the development prospects or even oddity of the endeavor Brush et al. (2009).

Conjugal Status and Family Responsibilities: In inspecting family duties regarding ladies business people, we perceive that family courses of action contrast in India from profoundly industrialized nations. In India, the social standard manages that youthful couples live with the spouse's family as a more distant family, which includes shared local and money related obligations. Besides, upper and center salary family units approach modest work to help with family unit and childcare tasks.

Notwithstanding the assorted family foundations, a significant number of ladies business people (85 percent) originate from families in which guardians were profoundly engaged with either giving or upholding to social administrations. Guardians, as good examples, are profoundly compelling in forming the estimations of social equity among the ladies business visionaries. Parental impact, they guarantee, "caused me to choose to do social work and volunteer." "Hence, in the non-benefit area, the human capital (impact) of guardians' contrasts from the revenue driven segment, where the guardians give abilities and encounters of running a revenue driven undertaking.

A sense towards autonomous basic leadership on their life and vocation is the inspirational factor behind this inclination of ladies turning out to be world business visionaries. The ladies of today are not any more slanted towards profession arrangement, advancement, plans and improvement alongside their kind of conceived task family, home and culture. The investigation by Rani (1996) found that the accessibility of relaxation time inspired ladies business visionaries from higher pay classes. In spite of the abovementioned, ladies business people are compelled to take enterprise without some other methods for adding to family salary D'Cruz (2003).The examination additionally found that, family backing and consolations are the most noteworthy encouraging element which helped ladies yearn for business. Pillai and Anna, (1990): An investigation delineated the way that portrayal of ladies business visionaries of Asian district in SMEs is generally low because of components like low degree of training, absence of capital and social or strict requirements. Nonetheless, the investigation uncovered that the majority of the ladies business people in SMEs are from the class of constrained business people looking for better family earnings.

Expanded backing ought to be given by the Government to help ladies business people so as to beat the difficulties looked by them. Ladies business visionaries additionally require support from their family and society. They ought to be given simple money related assistance without putting unreasonable conditions by banks and budgetary organizations. In the event that ladies business people get backing and consolation from family, society, government and money related organizations. Such positive exertion can open new roads for them and increment the attractiveness and gainfulness of business possessed by them. On the off chance that the issues of ladies business visionaries are tended to appropriately, they can develop as effective business visionaries much better than men business people.

Socio-Legal Factors

A social Legal factor is the blend among law and society. The legislature or higher specialists pass that would affect how organizations are demolished. For instance if the legislatures pass a law that there ought to be no kid work and anybody or business that conflicts with this law would be arraigned. The term social components allude to the realities and encounters that impact or control an individual' character, frames of mind and way of life. These variables help an individual live well in amicability with others in the general public.

Another significant factor to be contemplated is the help gotten from the legislature of Malaysia. While the administration has embraced different endeavors in advancing enterprise particularly among the ladies, there are more to be practiced. The strategy creators should proceed with their endeavors in sustaining more ladies business people and furthermore to encourage their prosperity. An arrangement that is cordial to new firms must be instituted. These incorporate evacuating imperatives, for example, red-tapes and to improve the permitting prerequisites. Progressively budgetary help are required in different structures, for example, pre-seed and seed financing so as to bring more ladies into enterprise. It is likewise essential to urge enormous organizations to have business joint efforts with SMEs and to encourage SMEs' development as they go universal. Without these backings, the endeavors in making quality, versatile and effective ladies business visionaries in all divisions of the economy would be lumbering. Given a favorable situation and sufficient support, Malaysian ladies business visionaries can understand their maximum capacity and boost their commitment to the nation's financial improvement. Ladies non-administrative associations (NGOs) and gatherings should organize with the goal that data on government help accessible explicitly for ladies business visionaries can be separated down.

Ladies business visionaries need to have an intense comprehension of the pioneering direction with the end goal for them to prevail in their endeavors.

These directions, including certainty, fearlessness, solid self-discipline, chance taking, inventiveness and creativity, etc. can be implanted inside the ladies business people through short courses, preparing programs, tutoring or even long haul courses prompting the honor of a recognition or degree. This is the place the administration organizations and affiliations assume a significant job in sustaining these aptitudes inside the ladies business visionaries.

Motivators as annual duty alleviation, limited or complimentary affiliation participation and preparing could form fruitful ladies business people.

Significant changes in ladies' lives are an immediate consequence of the intercession of non-administrative associations (NGOs). Numerous NGOs that manage the lightening of neediness for ladies regularly likewise center on backing for ladies' privileges just as giving administrations to ladies. Carr, Chen, and Jhabvala: (1996). In spite of the fact that enactment in India ensures and advances ladies' privileges much of the time, NGO mediation helps in implementing such rights. Sinha and Commuri, Mishra and Mishra (1998). Also, onlookers frequently credit the expansion of NGOs with effectively changing the political setting wherein ladies live and work Fisher (1998). In this examination, we inspect business engaged with starting such NGOs. Business enterprise, a much discussed subject, has been characterized in the revenue driven writing as "the reactant operator in the public eye which sets into movement new ventures, new mixes of creation and trade" Collins and Moore (1970).

According to the Human Development Report (2007), India positions 96th on the sex related improvement file of 137 countries. The sex strengthening measures, which gauge the degree of ladies support in the nation's monetary and political exercises, rank India as 110th of the 166 countries.

There are a few investigations supporting about guaranteeing collaboration among ladies related service, monetary service and social and welfare improvement service of the Government of India. The Planning commission just as the Indian government perceives the requirement for ladies to be a piece of the standard of financial improvement. Ladies business enterprise is viewed as a compelling technique to take care of the issues of provincial and urban neediness.

Business enterprise improvement for ladies is a significant factor in monetary advancement of India. Rustic ladies can be urged to begin bungalow businesses. Country based miniaturized scale endeavors have been empowered by the administration by different plans, for example, Integrated Rural Development Program (IRDP), Training of Rural Youth for Self Employment (TRYSEM), and Development of Women and Children in Rural Areas (DWCRA).The point is to expel destitution through enterprising projects. The endeavors of government and its various offices are capably enhanced by NGOs that are assuming a similarly significant job in encouraging ladies strengthening.

Regardless of deliberate endeavors of governments and NGOs there are sure holes. Obviously we have progressed significantly in enabling ladies yet the future adventure is troublesome and requesting. Ladies business visionaries are not forgotten about from the procedure of national and monetary advancement, especially in significant areas, for example, data and correspondences innovation (ICT) and bio-innovation, all together for the nation to effectively figure it out

Vision 2020. In any case, in view of Gem's examination on pioneering condition (Malaysia), the outcomes thought about ineffectively the administration's presentation, guaranteeing that its arrangements disapproval new firms, and the administration organization and guideline and authorizing necessities block new firms from growing. It raised questions about the administration's skill and adequacy in supporting new and developing firms. The investigation singled out the absence of monetary help, nature of instruction and preparing, and generally advertise receptiveness as other primary variables keeping down Malaysian business people Gatsiounis (2006).

Socio-Organization Factors:

The latest investigation that investigated a hereditary reason for extraordinary traits of ladies in social capacity and sympathy suggest a superior execution of organizations' made and run by ladies in view of their capacity to discuss better with representatives, providers and clients. Valencia, (2006).Women does work any other way from men. As indicated by Heffernan (2003), female arranging styles have been demonstrated to appear as something else and it has been shown that they are altogether increasingly advantageous to long haul business achievement.

Components identified with the craving to accomplish adaptability among work and family lives are esteemed distinctively by the sexual orientations. Cinnamon& Rich, (2002) Stephens and Felman, (1997). Likewise, Hisrich and Brush (1987) found that individual inspirations and proprietor/author objectives are identified with execution in ladies possessed organizations where opportunity inspiration was identified with endurance and autonomy was related with "no development".

Nordin's examination (2005) uncovered that the mental intentions, for example, smugness and the quest for freedom and steady ecological factors, for example, industry part and wellspring of fund influence ladies business visionaries from Terengganu in endeavoring into organizations.

Hisrich and Brush (1985) investigated to discover the purposes behind beginning the business by ladies business visionaries. Most much of the time referred to were 'push' variables of disappointment and weariness in their past occupations, trailed by enthusiasm for the business, with 'pull' factors, for example, self-rule an inaccessible third. The examination by Sullivan, Halbrendt, Wang, and Scannell

(1997) found that ladies see workplaces in enormous associations as essentially increasingly threatening and this discernment was identified with ladies' turnover aims. In this manner, 'push' elements might be a more significant impact for ladies than for men.

As of late, the 'biased based impediment'– the apparently invulnerable hindrance that anticipates female mid-supervisors from climbing to the official suite has become the focal point of consideration for the scientists Greene, Gatewood, &Carter (2001). Predictable with the examination of Hisrich and Brush (1985), these accomplished ladies who leave the enormous association to become business visionaries might be leaving their corporate situations because of the unattainable rank, in actuality a hierarchical push help.

A couple of studies analyzing ladies' entrance to capital utilized an exploratory structure system to decide if ladies confronted snags in getting bank credits. This exploration found that loaning organizations saw ladies entrepreneurs to be less fruitful than men. Buttner and Rosen (1988), Buttner and Rosen (1992) inferred that ladies were bound to property the forswearing of a bank credit to sex inclination than were men, however there was proof that a portion of the distinctions depended on the sexual orientation generalizations held by the capital suppliers. Ladies entrepreneurs were additionally essentially bound to see ill-bred treatment by loaning officials Fabowale, Orser, and Riding (1995). Institutional courses of action outline not just what number of ladies see openings and settle on key decisions, yet additionally how these ladies and others see their organizations. Especially appropriate is the means by which the 'gatekeepers' of assets just as the power holders, be it in the family unit and network or at the more extensive cultural levels, have an effect, regularly inconspicuous or covered up, on the enterprising action of ladies .Brush Bruin& Welter(2009).

Ladies business people have specialist related issues, for example, work non-attendance, absence of talented work, trouble in holding workforce and low profitability of work .Ganesan, Kaur, and Maheswari (2002) Nigam and Sharma (1997). Absence of monetary help makes issues for buy crude material and other infrastructural offices to begin their endeavors Starcher (1996).

Along these lines, almost certainly, the lady business visionary of a NGO managing socially delicate and dubious issues is an informed person who originates from a center to upper-salary family unit. Being of high station and profoundly taught, she is regarded and can practice control and prepare assets.

Rivalry from Male Entrepreneurs: Competition from male partners creates obstacles to ladies business visionaries in business the board procedure. Ladies business visionaries need to confront the limitations of rivalry from male business visionaries because of less hierarchical aptitudes than men.

Absence of Education and Awareness: Entrepreneurs must know about most recent mechanical changes; know how, and so forth for running business productively. In any case, it needs elevated level of instruction among business people. In a nation like India, the proficiency pace of ladies is found at low level contrasted with male populace. Along these lines, they have not adequate information on innovations; know how, and so on that influence their business adventures unfavorably.

Generation Problem: Production in an assembling endeavor includes coordination of various exercises. While a portion of these exercises are in the control of business person, there are others over which she has little control. Inappropriate coordination or unintended delay in execution of any movement is going to mess creation up in the business.

Absence of Knowledge of Availability of Raw Materials: For running business, business visionary requires to know about elective wellspring of crude material accessibility and high dealings abilities.

Ladies business visionaries have absence of such information and aptitudes which influence their business undertakings.

Low Level of Risk Taking Attitude: One pre-essential of the pioneering achievement is chance taking. It is ordinarily accepted that ladies being women's activist sexual orientation have generally safe taking capacity. Along these lines, they are stifled by the secured condition and are not enabled more often than not to go out on a limb regardless of whether she has ability to hold up under it. Cohoon, Wadhwa and Mitchell, (2010), present a point by point investigation of men &women business visionary's inspirations, foundation and encounters. The investigation depends on the information gathered from effective ladies business visionaries.

Out of them 59% had established at least two organizations. The examination distinguishes top five monetary and mental components inspiring ladies to become business visionaries. These are want to manufacture the riches, the desire to underwrite possess business thoughts they had, the intrigue of startup culture, a long standing want to claim their very own organization and working with another person didn't advance them.

The difficulties are more related with business as opposed to sexual orientation. Be that as it may, the examination finished up with the prerequisite of further examination like why ladies are such a great amount of worried about securing scholarly capital than their partner. Tutoring is essential to ladies, which gives consolation and money related help of colleagues, encounters and all around created proficient system.

Enterprise is considered as one of the most significant variables adding to the monetary advancement of the general public. There are confirmations to accept that nations which have proportionately higher level of business visionaries in their populace have grown a lot quicker when contrasted with nations, which have lesser level of them in the general public. In India, ladies comprise around 48 percent of the populace yet their investment in the financial exercises is just 34 percent. According to the Human Development Report (2007), India positions 96th on the sexual orientation related advancement list of 137 countries. The sexual orientation strengthening measures, which gauge the degree of ladies support in the nation's financial and political exercises, rank India as 110th of the 166 countries. In the rising complex social situation ladies have an urgent task to carry-out.

Cultural-Religious Issue:

Culture refers to the cumulative deposit of knowledge, experience, beliefs, values, attitudes, meanings, hierarchies, religion, notions of time, roles, spatial relations, concepts of the universe, and material objects and possessions acquired by a group of people in the course of generations through individual and group striving. Culture is the systems of knowledge shared by a relatively large group of people's.

What cultural factors mean?

In an engineered situation, Synthetic Psychological Environment alludes to the portrayal of impacts to people and gatherings because of culture. The faith in and love of a super-human controlling force, particularly an individual God or divine beings. A religion is a sorted out assortment of convictions, social frameworks, and world sees that relate mankind to a request for presence.

Sexual orientation Roles in Shari 'at Islam - According to dynamic Indonesian Islamic researchers, for example, K.H.Hussein Muhammad (He is the chief of the

Islamic live-in school 'Dar al-Tauhid Arjawinaangun' in Cirebon, West Java, and the executive for talk improvement at Rahima (Center for Training and Information on Islam and Women's Rights Issues. He is additionally dynamic with the non-government association 'Puan Amal Hayati') neither the Qur'an nor "Hadiths" disallow ladies to work in the open circle. Islam doesn't give limits for the spots where ladies and men can and should work. Each separately can and may work in or outside the home and in any appropriate zone, which is required so as to endure.

Numerous Ulama (Islamic pastorate) allude to refrain 34 from the letter of A Nisa as a contention for sponsorship up male predominance over ladies and as an explanation, why ladies ought not be associated with open exercises and why they can't be pioneers: "Men are the defenders and maintainers of ladies, since God has given the one more (quality) than the other, and on the grounds that they bolster them from their methods". In "Surat al-Ahzab" 34, it is expressed that ladies should remain at home. Nonetheless, in different stanzas of the Qur'an and "Hadiths", it is expressed that ladies and men share equivalent rights and openings in the open circle (At-Taubah 71).

K.H. Hussein Muhammad brings up that considering all stanzas of the Qur'an related with ladies, there isn't one content that communicates particularly that no one but men can become open pioneers. There is additionally no refrain in the Qur'an that says men are physically and mentally more fit than females.

Prof. Dr. Al Yasa Abubakar, leader of the Syari'at Office in Banda Aceh, contends inside the "Syari'at" guidelines in Aceh ladies are approved similarly as men to make a move in the open circle just as in legislative issues. Not with standing , he accept that ladies as a result of their family duties feel more secure, on the off chance that they can remain at home and stay away from open exercises. He pursues a similar line as K.H. Hussein Muhammad, when he says that in his understanding

Islam gives equivalent chances to people. Moreover, he expresses that, if in everyday life the space for open exercises (in governmental issues, the economy, and so on.) given to ladies is littler than for men, this isn't in rationality with Islam, yet identified with the recognition and propensities for the populace.

Prof. Dr. Al Yasa Abu-Bakr, states that ladies' just as men's privileges are similarly offset with their separate obligations in the Qur'an. As indicated by Prof. Dr. Al Yasa Abu-Bakr, except if it is as of now concurred before the marriage, the spouse doesn't reserve the privilege to preclude his significant other to play out a financial movement. Besides, he says that most of strict pioneers concur that in the event of any explanation the spouse can't work or can't totally satisfy his family salary gaining obligation, the wife must work. K.H. Hussein Muhammad and other dynamic Islamic researchers, contend that Islam is an extremely dynamic religion for ladies, was profoundly libertarian for now is the ideal time, and remains so in a portion of its Scriptures. They battle that Islamic law has advanced in manners that are unfriendly to sexual orientation balance not on the grounds that it obviously pointed toward that path, but since of specific translation by male centric pioneers and a blending of Islamic lessons with ancestral traditions and customs.

Not with standing that, it is likewise to be viewed as that the primary spouse of the Prophet Mohammad was a fruitful business visionary. Khadijah, the little girl of Khuwalid, had been hitched twice and bereft twice before she proposed to Muhammad, who was 15 years more youthful than her, and her worker. As per the content, his work execution and great business aptitudes were in certainty two of the fundamental reasons Khadija was pulled in to him. Khadija was well off and ready to give the family salary without anyone else's input. This enabled the prophet to spread his confidence.

Caste System

To comprehend the importance of position as a social impact, we quickly portray the station framework in India society was separated into four classifications of people: Brahmins, Kshatriyas, Vaishyas, and Shudras. Participation in the position got genetic and fixed forever.

Such division clarified wide contrasts among demeanors, practices, and inclinations.

An individual's name and calling normally signal the person's position, and however urbanization and administrative changes have rendered names and callings less recognizable, rank still remains attributed. Ladies are frequently forced into callings recommended by standing through cultural standards that strengthen their frames of mind and desires.

A various leveled and stable standing framework unequivocally impacts and compels ladies' decision and doesn't allow a Vaishya to achieve the calling of a cleric, which is held for Brahmins. Position consequently turns into a social determinant that frequently clarifies the decision (or deficiency in that department) of the individual's calling.

Nonetheless, since the 1960s and 1970s, this impact is fading. Regardless of enactment banning certain strict and conventional practices, for example, widow consuming and endowment, and not withstanding guidelines elevating governmental policy regarding minorities in society to counter the impacts of position, a lady's life remains affected by the strict custom of subjection to the male individuals from the family.

In India, the lady of the hour's family can wind up owing debtors and neediness in the wake of giving an endowment of gold, money and different advantages for the husband-to-be's family. On the off chance that a guaranteed endowment doesn't appear, a lady of the hour may endure pitilessness and misuse. Hinduism puts an extraordinary accentuation on a lady's subjection to the men in the family—father, spouse, and children—at various stages throughout everyday life. A lady's life is additionally influenced by the station into which she is conceived, impacting who she weds, her occupation, her monetary prosperity, and even her opportunity of development.

A lady's class, a result of station to an enormous degree, unequivocally influences her chances for a training. For instance, ladies naturally introduced to the Brahmin standing, for the most part compared with the scholarly and holy class, may not become clerics however are required to be taught and can without much of a stretch partake in expert, social, and social life. This thus converts into benefit and status. High rank likewise offers her the chance to wed into first class groups 'of glory, riches, and status. Lower position ladies, particularly country ladies, don't approach instruction and different assets and are frequently less liberated from male subjection than the higher taught and higher standing ladies. Pay and station are commonly related, interceded by access to instruction and social capital. Be that as it may, the late 1980s and mid 1990s have seen restricted upward portability of lower standings because of governmental policy regarding minorities in society plans Assayag (1995).

Almost 80 percent Brahmins recommends that specific elements may make it likely that ladies of higher stations are pulled in to, and are effective at, NGO business enterprise in India. Sober minded reasons of societal position make higher standing ladies bound to have the ability to battle customary powers and legitimize socially questionable issues identified with ladies. We find that lower position ladies organizers may have noteworthy instructive foundations that may make up for their lower status when managing neighborhood specialists and acquiring assets.

Hinduism is the religion of most of the number of inhabitants in India be that as it may, a critical minority populace (23 percent) comprises of Muslims, Christians, Sikhs, etc. In spite of the fact that the larger part of our examples are Hindus, our respondent's didn't offer religion as an inspiration for or a factor in their activities. This is as opposed to Gupta (1991), who recommends that religion, is a significant factor in clarifying revenue driven business in India.

Given a little and geologically restricted example, we can't state whether our discoveries on standing and religion demonstrate a pre-ponderance of one strict gathering or position among ladies business visionaries if the discoveries are illustrative of the populace. Nonetheless, our discoveries do demonstrate that rank (and perhaps religion) ought to be additionally examined as potential determinants of business enterprise in India.

In India, regardless of the numerous endeavors to free society of the consequences of the position framework, the framework keeps on working unobtrusively (and not all that quietly) at numerous levels. The first class in India are regularly the informed Brahmins, the Brahmin being the most noteworthy standing. They appreciate certain benefits of social associations among themselves and are regarded as pioneers and savvy people.

Traditional Culture

The customary jobs of housewives are continuously changing into ladies business people with the progression of time. The ladies are presently increasingly slanted towards sorted out auxiliary work which not the slightest bit hampers the customary angles. Numerous individuals accept that the females will in general lose their obligations toward their customary objectives. Be that as it may, the truth of the matter is that the females turning business visionaries are substantially more systematized towards taking care of different employments at the same time. It might get repetitive for anybody however not our road savvy ladies.

Family Related

From the natural point of view, family impact, especially parental impact has been found as the forerunner of private company profession intrigue.

Relatives, particularly guardians assume a key job in setting up the attractive quality and validity of pioneering activity for people. Scherer et al. (1989) found that the nearness of a parent innovative good example was related with a person's business execution. People with a parent innovative good example were seen to be superior workers and were altogether not quite the same as people without pioneering good examples, who were seen to be low entertainers. Most of fruitful ladies business visionaries recognized one parent as being progressively powerful, that is, numerous effective ladies distinguish emphatically with their dads. Henning &Jardim (1978) and Belcourt et al's. (1991) study revealed that 33 percent of Canadian ladies business visionaries overviewed expressed their dads were business visionaries. This is sensible as parent-kid relationship advances accomplishment endeavoring and freedom .Stein &Bailey (1973).

Female work power support additionally is by all accounts identified with the frame of mind of the family towards ladies. Aminah (1998), for example, in an investigation of chose effective profession ladies in Malaysia, uncovered that changing frames of mind of guardians and spouses towards an increasingly positive pattern were seen to be identified with higher instructive accomplishment of ladies which thusly could impact ladies' support in the work power by setting up their very own organizations.

Additionally, the life partners assume significant jobs in urging their innovative spouses to join and partake in the exercises of these affiliations. In contrast to religions, women's activist philosophy is overwhelmingly offered as the spurring and legitimizing factor. Our business visionaries show a profound and long haul duty to women's activist belief system. A significant number of them were engaged with social developments and went to their women's activist convictions during this time, others built up their belief system through working environment experience and at home. Enterprising ladies in the revenue driven division in the west additionally frequently consider themselves to be women's activists who embrace eccentric jobs

Brush, (1992) Fischer, Reuber, and Dyke (1993) Allen and Truman (1993) Moore and Buttner (1997).Although women's liberation is a general idea, the social and authentic setting in India offers ascend to specific divergences in the significance of abuse and social equity. Gedal of (1999), Niranjana, (1998) John, (1998). Women's activist belief system, as our respondents get it, perceives this distinction as is clear in their anxiety for the persecution of lower position ladies frequently coming about because of the qualities and standards held in the public eye. For instance, they were insightful of the issues looked by poor lower standing provincial ladies because of the conventional social and political organizations that perceive and regularly advance the subjection of the ladies to male relatives. This mindfulness, joined with their experience and philosophy, prodded them to plan something for mitigate the issues of ladies.

Besides, the components influencing ladies business enterprise are fundamentally inward assets: training and experience just as social, family, and social associations.

Customary outside assets that are significant for revenue driven ladies business people, for example, advances, have little sway on non-benefit ladies business visionaries. Money related soundness in the family and family support is fundamental for most ladies in tightening the crucial the NGO.

Socio-social Disturbance: Women need to oversee both home and business obligations one after another. Such commitments may turn into an extraordinary obstruction for certain ladies in prevailing as a business person. Parental good examples and early expert and volunteer experience served to raise their mindfulness and persuade a large number of these ladies to pioneer enterprise to seek after social equity since they are self-pronounced women's activists.

Some other basic reasons or causes

Portability Constraint: The Indian culture is a traditionalist society which confines the versatility of ladies business visionaries. Ladies are less portable than men. The certainty to travel day and night and to various areas and States is inadequate in ladies contrasting and men.

Different Constraints: They are poor mental self-view of ladies, insufficient inspiration, separating treatment, absence of opportunity of articulation, and so on.

The rule factor in creating business among ladies isn't regarding foundation or budgetary help or distinguishing an endeavor yet it is an issue of clearing the ground for their development into enterprise. For a long time together they have been bound to an optional job and limited to the homes and you need to bring out with the goal that they become independent, self-regarding venturesome individuals. In spite of the fact that there are a few variables adding to the rise of ladies as business people, the continued and composed exertion from all measurements would prepare for the ladies moving into innovative action accordingly adding to the social and financial improvement of the individuals from the family and along these lines picking up uniformity and equivalent significance for themselves.

The customary jobs of housewives are bit by bit changing into ladies business people. A portion of the components answerable for these progressions are better training, changing socio social esteems and requirement for strengthening pay. At the point when appropriate presentation, training and information are conferred to them, Indian ladies will demonstrate themselves to be exceptionally potential profitable power for the improvement of the country.

Organizational-Cultural Issues

Hisrich and Brush (1987) recommended that emotionally supportive networks, coaches, and guides; business partners and companions; cooperation in exchange affiliations and ladies' gatherings are the critical systems which are decidedly connected with business execution. As per Fraser (1995) and Wheeler (1995), the utilization of casual tutoring steady connections is probably the most ideal methods for setting up a business and these connections helped the new business person sidestep the impediments which hinder development, achievement, and

Individual satisfaction. The exhibition of ladies business people in their organizations has become a significant region of late arrangement and scholarly discussion. Similarly minimal thorough and top to bottom research, Not withstanding, has been attempted on the issues of sexual orientation and business execution. Execution is the demonstration of performing, of accomplishing something effectively, utilizing information as recognized from simply having it.

Nonetheless, execution is by all accounts conceptualized, operationalized and estimated in various ways .Srinivasan (1994), therefore making cross correlation troublesome. Among the most as often as possible utilized operationalization are endurance, development in representatives, and productivity .Lerner, Brush, &Hisrich (1997).Women who attempt to enter an industry, either in an administrative or innovative job, are commonly presented to different natural imperatives. Beginning and working business includes significant hazard and exertion with respect to the business visionary, especially in the light of most noteworthy disappointment rate. Maybe, this rate is considerably higher on account of ladies business people who need to confront the standard business issues as well as their family issues. This not just restricts the extent of their commitment to the industrialization procedure, yet in addition undermines the beneficial usage of an accessible human asset, that is generally required in our nation Rajani (2008).

Are there any basic and social components important to ladies' business enterprise of NGOs? NGOs in the territory of Maharashtra in India, where ladies assume a significant job in NGOs identified with sexual orientation issues .Jani and Pedroni (1997).Entrepreneurs in the two areas face comparative difficulties: recognizing openings, advancing imaginative thoughts, executing thoughts into practical ventures, preparing assets, and undertaking dangers inborn in beginning another task. Besides, business visionaries in the two parts are similarly powerless against the individual, basic, and social situations in which they live. Besides, there are contrasts in the impacts of different factors based on the sort of associations benefit or non-benefit.

Concentrates done in less industrialized nations by Berger (1991), Gupta (1991), Shabbir and Di Gregorio (1996), and Naffziger and Terrell (1996), we locate that social qualities and standards are basic in clarifying business enterprise.

This writing recommends that the person's choice to begin a business is influenced by variables, for example, family support, capabilities, business experience, and financial and character Qualities.

In spite of the fact that these investigations depend on business people of revenue driven undertakings, we anticipate that a large number of these variables should impact non-benefit business visionaries also. Notwithstanding the elements referenced in the revenue driven writing, writing recommends that non-benefit business visionaries are driven by their convictions, individual encounters, view of network needs, and want to give administrations to other people. They are as likely concerning benefit business visionaries to be eager to go out on a limb, self-coordinated, and inventive.

Nonetheless, their attention is on what they can accomplish for other people. Young, (1983), Pilz (1995) Bilodeau and Slivinski (1996) Kassam, Handy, and Ranade (2000).

On account of social molding, ladies are disheartened to build up the limit of versatility and certainty required for showcasing capacity. Along these lines, they fall behind in this space.

Rivalry from Male Entrepreneurs: Competition from male partners creates obstacles to ladies business visionaries in business the executives' procedure. Ladies business visionaries need to confront the requirements of rivalry structure male business visionaries because of less authoritative aptitudes than men.

Creation Problem: Production in an assembling venture includes coordination of various exercises. While a portion of these exercises are in the control of business person, there are others over which she has little control. Inappropriate coordination or unintended delay in execution of any movement is going to mess creation up in the business.

The field of business visionaries isn't simple, particularly on account of ladies. Other than numerous positive perspectives, these other sexual orientation warm blooded animals need to confront issues in the facades as well. The impediments in the development of ladies enterprise are predominantly absence of cooperation with effective business visionaries, social un-acknowledgment as ladies business people, family duty, sex separation, missing system, low need given by brokers to give advance to ladies business visionaries.

To know the reasons because of which the female foundations are influenced in the market of business, we have to know the interchange of limitations and openings influencing female enterprise in creating nations like India.

2.6. SELF-EFFICACY AND WOMEN ENTREPRENEURS

The construct of self-efficacy is also relevant for promoting health behaviors. How much effort an individual expends and how long they persist in the face of obstacles is determined by their beliefs about the consequences of their behavior and their beliefs about their ability to perform specific behaviors in certain situations (Bandura, 1982). Bandura argued that perceived self-efficacy for a given situation or behavior emerges from an individual integrating all of the information they have about the situation.

Women's leadership in contexts of small business ownership can be argued to present different models of leadership style, values, and challenges than those developed by women in organizational leadership roles. Recent studies of women in business ownership (i.e. Business Development Bank of Canada, 1999; Industry Canada, 1999) suggest that these women business owner-leaders exercise a large degree of control over the vision and purpose of the enterprise, and often deliberately craft working environments and cultures that support their personal values and preferences. They can cultivate their own working relationships with greater freedom. They can seek as much challenge and take as much risk as they can personally manage. For some women, these freedoms come at a high cost of fears and insecurities, unpredictable workload and isolation (Canadian Advisory Council, 1991). In sum, small business ownership creates leadership issues for women that are different in kind than those shared by their sisters in senior management positions located in corporate or government settings.

A growing body of literature is emerging to study the phenomenon of women's leadership as small business owners along a wide variety of dimensions, drawing from perspectives ranging from market models of business economic development to women's psychological development and feminist studies of women's leadership. Qualitative studies in the past five years have indicated contested issues related to values, identity and the meaning of leadership emerging in this trend of women business ownership (Gay, 1997; Robertson, 1997; Thrasher and Smid, 1998). For example, women don't always accept the dominant formula that success equals money and power. Women who start their own business sometimes do so to craft a new way of working, and many continue to fight barriers related to traditional constructs of economic power and expectations. Many women business owners claim that the whole experience changes them profoundly.

Women business owners' psychological characteristics were a focus of many early studies (Hisrich and Brush, 1987; Watkins and Watkins, 1983), showing the historical interest in relationships between psychological profile and leadership success. More recently, studies of women's personal development and change related to their small business leadership experiences is a recurring theme. These tend to highlight the importance of women's struggles with identity and personal change in leading their own business, including shaping their own role in the venture (Albert, 1992; Fenwick, 1998; MacKeracher, 1996; Wells. 1998).

Women's motives for starting and leading a business have been documented in many studies (Lee and Rogoff, 1997; NFWBO, 1999b) to help illuminate the desires and needs of women leaders who choose business ownership over organizational management positions. Women's reasons for business start-up reasons encompass a wide range: desiring greater work-life flexibility, seeking challenge, fulfilling a long-felt desire, or escaping an organizational glass ceiling.

Rob Hallak et al.(2013) The results found that place identity (sense of identity with their town of residence) was positively related to entrepreneurial self-efficacy (beliefs in their capabilities as entrepreneurs). Furthermore, self-efficacy is a direct driver of performance, and not vice versa, for both male and female entrepreneurs. However, multigroup invariance analysis suggests that the nonrecursive model is partially moderated by the entrepreneurs' gender. The relationship between entrepreneurial self-efficacy and performance was significantly greater for the male group. The findings have implications for scholars in tourism and entrepreneurial studies, and for policy makers trying to support the sustainable development of tourism destinations

Koçak, Akin et al. (2013) Social cognitive theory is used as the theoretical framework in this study. The results showed that social capital plays a significant role in affecting opportunity recognition in both countries. Self-efficacy effects vary across the cases and the two countries. Culture has a significant role in mediating the effect of self-efficacy.

Babak (2012) results showed that Pakistani female entrepreneurs were found to exhibit many similarities in issues with other female entrepreneurs in developing countries. The findings indicated that factors like "Lack of finance, Restriction on mobility, Limited decision making, Lack of role models and guiders, Men's hold on markets, Family pressure and Discrimination are major barriers in the way of entrepreneurialism. Also showed that the female entrepreneurs in Pakistan are very important to economic and social development but they are facing serious troubles. Women's entrepreneurship, properly exploited, has great potential as a tool for transforming Pakistani economy. In conclusion, the results of this study proved that the in Pakistan women's entrepreneurial activities are not only a means for economic survival but also have positive social repercussions for the women themselves, their families and their social environment.

Frances M. Amatucci & Daria C. Crawley (2011) findings showed that only partially attest to the lack of confidence combined with anxiety about dealing with financial management. Age and racial differences are significantly related to financial self-efficacy (FSE).

Cohoon, Wadhwa & Mitchell (2010) present a detailed exploration of men & women Entrepreneur's motivations, background and experiences. The study is based on the data collected from successful women entrepreneurs. Out of them 59% had founded two or more companies. The study identifies top five financial & psychological factors motivating women to become entrepreneurs. These are desire to build the wealth, the wish to capitalize own business ideas they had, the appeal of startup culture, a long standing desire to own their own company and working with someone else did not appeal them. The challenges are more related with entrepreneurship rather than gender. However, the study concluded with the requirement of further investigation like why women are so much concerned about protecting intellectual capital than their counterpart. Mentoring is very important to women, which provides encouragement & financial support of business partners, experiences & well developed professional network.

Tambunan (2009) The study focused mainly on women entrepreneurs in small and medium enterprises based on data analysis and review of recent key literature. This study found that in Asian developing countries SMEs are gaining overwhelming importance; more than 95% of all firms in all sectors on average per country. The study also depicted the fact that representation of women entrepreneurs in this region is relatively low due to factors like low level of education, lack of capital and cultural or religious constraints. However, the study revealed that most of the women entrepreneurs in SMEs are from the category of forced entrepreneurs seeking for better family incomes.

Petridou et al. (2008) appraise rural women entrepreneurs running co-operatives in Greece to examine the effects of training support on their entrepreneurial skills and attitudes, co-operatives' viability and growth prospects, and work-family balance. Their study illustrates that participants perceived training positively in terms of skill improvements, identification and capturing of business opportunities, effective co-operation and flexibility in decision making, more positive attitudes towards entrepreneurship, development and growth prospects for the cooperative and better work-family balance.

Lisowska (2002) argued that various religious, social, and historical stereotypical beliefs about the typical occupational paths for men versus women and practices engrained in traditional socialization processes hinder women entrepreneurs. In particular, she suggested that some of these beliefs included the superstitious notion that the land will not produce yields if cultivated by women and the traditional identification of certain clusters of competencies for women different to that of men. In the case of cluster of competencies, women were generally perceived to be expressive, emotional, and hesitative while men were perceived to be more assertive, objective, and reckless. Linked this theoretically to the low levels of self-efficacy that these women hold and the absence of institutional and cultural processes that engendered them. Given the above contended that there „is an overall lack of social acceptance for women in private economic activity. Collectively, these studies put forward the case that traditional social expectations, as it pertains to gender disparities in labor market participation and/or aspirations, explain gendered entrepreneurial patterns. These studies therefore suggest that internalized notions of appropriate labor market engagement and the low levels of entrepreneurial efficacy on the part of women warrant further investigation.

Das (2000) performed a study on women entrepreneurs of SMEs in two states of India, viz, Tamilnadu and Kerala. The initial problems faced by women entrepreneurs are quite similar to those faced by women in western countries. However, Indian women entrepreneurs faced lower level of work-family conflict and are also found to differ from their counterparts in western countries on the basis of reasons for starting and succeeding in business. Similar trends are also found in other Asian countries such as Indonesia and Singapore. Again the statistics showed that the proportion of business setup and operated by women is much lower than the figures found in western countries.

Caruana, Morris, and Vella (1998), in their study of Maltese export firms, found that women and men business owners show similarity in demonstrating three characteristics deemed key for business owners: innovativeness (creative ability to create purposeful change or develop novel products, services, and processes); risk-taking (active willingness to pursue opportunity notwithstanding reasonable chance of costly failure); and proactiveness (the perseverance, adaptability, and assertiveness to initiate rather than react to the environment, and do whatever it takes to bring the venture to fruition). Masters and Meier (1988) found women's entrepreneurial risk-taking to be almost as high as men's, although they did not consider respondents' personal meanings of what constitutes risk in a particular situation. Sexton and Bowman-Upton (1990) found that in comparison to men, women have higher willingness to accept change and greater need for autonomy while having lower energy levels and risk-taking propensities.

Bowen & Hisrich (1986) compared & evaluated various research studiesdone on Entrepreneurship including women entrepreneurship. It summaries various studies in this way that female entrepreneurs are relatively well educated in general but perhaps not in management skills, high in internal locus of control, more masculine, or instrumental than other women in their values likely to have had entrepreneurial fathers, relatively likely to have first born or only children, unlikely to start business in traditionally male dominated industries & experiencing a need of additional managerial training. Women network report on Women in Business & in Decision Making focus on women entrepreneurs, about their problems in starting & running the business, family back ground, education, size of business unit. Some interesting facts which came out from this report are less educated women entrepreneurs are engaged in micro enterprises, have husband & children but have no help at home. Most of the women establish enterprises before the age of 35, after gaining some experience as an employee somewhere else. The motivational factors were desire for control & freedom to take their own decision as well as earning handsome amount of money. Dedication of more than 48 hours in a week with the family support to their enterprises gave them a sense of self confidence. However, to maintain balance between family & work life is a major challenge before women entrepreneurs especially for those who have children & working husband.

2.7. QUALITY OF LIFE AND WOMEN ENTREPRENEURS

Researchers of happiness and life satisfaction show that the level of subjective well-being is not much predicted and caused by objective economic factors. Veenhoven (1990) shows that people can be subjectively happy in an objectively bad condition, or feel unhappy in good ones. Pan, Zinkhan, and Sheng (2007) also suggest that economic growth has no effect on happiness. Much more effect on subjective well-being might be achieved when there is a positive impact on the factors which are directly linked to people's safety and security, meaningfulness of jobs and fluffiness in life, positive social relationships, and so on. These factors are related to social circumstances, and the more improvement people see in these areas, the happier they might be.

Policy makers improve economic and social environment by solving social problems.

Significant and quick changes in the social area, however, are hard to attain. Policy is limited to resources, and its effectiveness of directly impacting upon the subjective well-being of individuals and communities is not high. Current social and economic realities show that social policy fails to effectively meet the needs of various groups, and social change is slow. New solutions of how policy could contribute more to social change, which can have positive impact on the well-being of citizens, should be found in this context.

It is accepted that the level of subjective well-being changes in response to changed circumstances (OECD 2011). Thus, the level of subjective well-being may increase by improving a social environment. Social entrepreneurship is suggested to be an effective model of social development and change. This notion is supported by such authors as :

Nicholls (2006), who stress that social entrepreneurs influence social behavior for the good. The main areas in which social entrepreneurs create change are poverty alleviation through empowerment, health care, education, environmental preservation, sustainable development, etc. It is intuitively clear that social entrepreneurship relates to subjective well-being. The evidence of such a relationship, however, has not been determined enough. This encourages exploring the hypothesis that positive changes in social entrepreneurship could have a positive effect on subjective well-being of individuals and communities.

Veenhoven (1984) defines subjective well-being as the degree to which an individual judges the overall quality of her or his life as a whole in a favorable way. In order to explore subjective well-being, people are usually asked whether they are happy of satisfied with their life.

Lu et al. (2014) results showed that workers with statutory working hours, higher wages and less migrant experience had higher HRQOL scores. Need (contracting a disease in the past two weeks and perception of needing health service) had the greatest total effect on HRQOL ($\beta = -0.78$), followed by enabling (labor contract, insurance purchase, income, physical examination during work and training) ($\beta = 0.40$), predisposing (age, family separation, education) ($\beta = 0.22$) and health practices and use of health service (physical exercise weekly, health check-up and use of protective equipment) ($\beta = -0.20$).Priority should be given to satisfy the needs of migrant workers, and improve the enabling resources.

Vinita Sinha & Subramanian (2013) Quality of work life is the extent to which workers can satisfy important personal needs through their experiences in the organization. It focuses strongly on providing a work environment conducive to satisfy individual needs. It is assumed that if employees have more positive attitudes about the organization and their productivity increases The present piece of work was conducted to examine whether work related factors have any relationship with the perception of quality of work life and also to compare the relationship between quality of work life in total of 60 employees from private sector, public sector employees and entrepreneurs. This study examines the differences found between entrepreneurs, government and private association's employees' ratings of their quality of work life experience.

The results are thoroughly analysed and discussed. The results highlights that work related factors have significant and differential relationship with perception of quality of work life among three sectors.

Sulaksha Nayak, Harisha .G. Joshi (2013) study showed that Regular assessment of Quality of Work Life (QWL) can potentially provide organizations with important information about the welfare of their employees such as job satisfaction, work-family balance, job security and job stress. The global recession has led to the decline in the margins of the Indian IT industry as a result of which salaries of IT professionals have reduced and feelings of insecurity are increasing. The study highlights the fact that SME's particularly are at a disadvantage as they are unable to justify the best talents in the industry, owing to their limitations in infrastructure. Information Technology professionals are highly educated with high career aspirations and have a growing consciousness of their rights. Hence it is only imperative that organizations that employ them must be concerned about their quality of work life.

Krishnan, Latha & Kamalanabhan (2013) Many entrepreneurship researchers share the opinion that entrepreneurship is a positive force which enhances employment generation and promotes new products and services to meet the needs and wants of their clients. However, emphasis on entrepreneurship within micro enterprises is limited. Hence, an attempt was made to identify and assess entrepreneurial attitude orientation and competencies and skills among women entrepreneurs in micro enterprise leading to entrepreneurial success and ultimately life satisfaction. Multivariate analysis technique like Factor Analysis and Structural Equation Modeling (SEM) were conducted to identify the entrepreneurship success related factors. The findings showed a direct relationship between entrepreneurial attitudes related constructs and entrepreneurial competencies related factors, leading to entrepreneurial success, and life satisfaction among micro entrepreneurs.

Danabakyam, M & Swapna kurian (2012) Women Entrepreneurship plays a prime role in industrial development. India has always been a land of entrepreneurs and also occupied a strategic position in the Indian economy. Today the village and MSME units account for about 45% of the total industrial production, 30% of the country exports and estimated to employ 96millions person in over 26 million units throughout the country. The government of India has defined women entrepreneurship based on women participation in equity and employed of a business enterprise. The researcher has taken this topic to identify the industrial profile, to identify the motivating factors of women entrepreneurs and contributing factors to the success and to analyze the relationship between industries related factors and success of entrepreneurs. The researcher has been selected 100 respondents from in and around Chennai City by convenience sampling method. The percentage analysis, weighted average rank analysis and chi-square statistical methods are used for the study.

Svetlana Šajeva & Egidijus Rybakovas (2011) study revealed that researchers define social entrepreneurs as those who create social value by developing innovative solutions to social problems. Subjective well-being refers to people's personal evaluations of their lives. The relationship between social entrepreneurial activities and subjective well-being exists due to the fact that subjective well-being is highly dependent on social circumstances that, in turn, are positively influenced by social activities, provided by social entrepreneurs. A general hypothesis validated in this study is that a higher level of social entrepreneurship in a certain country conditions a higher level of subjective well-being.

Jindal (2005) The findings showed that 60.67 % respondents had no work related problems, 59.33 % had work related worries, 13.33 % had planned work according to urgency for completion of tasks. Only 14.67 % organized their work and made time plan as against 15.33 % who made no plans. 62.23 % were familiar with the supplies and equipment and 88 % knew the procedure for completing the work.

Kapadia & Barodia (2004) Women were often the main economic agents to ensure the survival of a poor family. Hence women get empowered if they are led towards entrepreneurship. They also report that there were successful women entrepreneurs today heading enterprises like electronics, multimedia, garment industry and so on. They also suggested that women entrepreneurs had to face many problems.

Patel (2004) found that women entrepreneurs operated in diverse economic and socio- political environment and therefore, they had diverse needs. It was further said that although some women successfully operated growth oriented enterprise and had enjoyed some advantages in certain female preferred sectors, they faced a range of interlinked and mutually reinforcing gender constraints at the household and institutional levels. It was found that majority of women began their enterprise to cope with rising cost of household subsistence. These women were locked into low investment, low growth and low profit activities, not only because of limited markets and enterprise opportunities in poor economics, but also due to gender inequalities.

Singh (2004) reported that women entrepreneurs had certain qualities like risk taking, innovativeness and self-confidence. The qualities of an entrepreneur in raising enterprise and their functioning leads to economic development of a country in different ways depending on how much innovative she was in carrying out the venture .It was found that they faced many problems which were results of political, social and economic interactions among various factors.

Chhichhia (2004) It was found that all entrepreneurs had some or the other problem. 91 % said that there was lack of training, 79 % entrepreneurs reported that they had family responsibilities and financial pressure, 54 % said that time spent did not give worthy outcome. 35 % said that there was a need of modification from time to time. 72 % reported that they had to struggle more to survive in the market. 93 % entrepreneur did not use internet in their enterprise, 3 % had complete organized computer set up in their enterprises.

Mehrotra (2003) It was observed that majority of the respondents from both rural and urban areas were highly affected by the general decline in financial position. A large majority, i.e., 80 % were always under constant financial stress in spite of copying strategies adopted by them. Rural families felt that these tasks were very tiring and stressful due to the non-availability of paid help. Further, 75 % of urban and 82 % rural families were either always or sometimes affected by psychological problems

Rao (2002) researched on problems of the women entrepreneurs. They classified the problems into personal, social and economic categories. Lack of experience, lack of business exposure, and conservative attitude towards risk were reported to be personal problems. Among social problems was male domination, unwritten rules of society and family responsibilities. Lack of economic power, no right over property, dependence on male members on banking and such others were the economic problems faced by women entrepreneurs. Among the socio- personal problems, 70 % faced lack of family and community support. 60 % had managerial experience. Production problem in the form of availability of land, plots and premises was faced by 70 % respondents. Lack of knowledge about marketing the product was the major problem faced by 76 % of the respondents. 74 % faced financial problems regarding loan and subsidy whereas inadequate government assistance was reported as problem by 70 % respondents.

2.8 ENTREPRENEURIAL SELF-EFFICACY (ESE)

Studies concentrating on innovative inspiration, aims and conduct commonly incorporate enterprising self-adequacy (ESE) as an illustrative variable. There are numerous components that impact an individual to seek after turning into a business visionary, which can be a mix of individual properties, qualities, foundation, experience and air (Krueger Jr and Brazeal 1994; Krueger Jr, Reilly et al. 2000; Shane, Locke et al. 2003; Baron 2004; Arenius and Minniti 2005). Among these individual characteristics do we find pioneering self-viability (ESE) as especially significant for foreseeing new pursuit expectations (Boyd and Vozikis 1994; Zhao, Seibert et al. 2005; Barbosa, Gerhardt et al. 2007). Enterprising self-adequacy is a develop estimating an individual's confidence in their capacity to effectively dispatch a pioneering adventure (McGee, Peterson et al. 2009). Enterprising self-adequacy fuses both character and natural factors and is believed to be a solid indicator of pioneering expectations and at last activity (Bird 1988; Boyd and Vozikis 1994).

Enterprising self-viability has developed as a promising build, with the possibility to anticipate pioneering execution and for improving the pace of innovative exercises through preparing and instruction (Mueller and Goic 2003; Zhao, Seibert et al. 2005; Florin, Karri et al. 2007). In any case, the develop remains exactly immature and numerous researchers have called for refinements of the build (Forbes 2005; Kolvereid and Isaksen 2006).

2.8.1. Measuring entrepreneurial self-efficacy (ESE)

The measure enterprising self-adequacy has been broadly received for recognizing pioneering expectations and subsequently innovative direct, and for exploring how instruction and preparing can be utilized to improve innovative activity. By and by, specialists experience issues arriving at agreement for how to utilize the measure. A few researchers (Chen, Gully et al. 2004) are of the assessment that it isn't important to have a space explicit enterprising self-adequacy build, and rather advocate the utilization of a general proportion of self-viability. Most researchers recognize the multi-dimensional nature of innovative self-viability develop (Zhao, Seibert et al. 2005; Wilson, Kickul et al. 2007), still an itemized assessment of the fundamental measurements stay unexplored. There are right now irregularities in how scientists approach catching the dimensionality of the pioneering self-viability build.

2.8.2. Dimensionality of entrepreneurial self-efficacy (ESE)

Uni-dimensional

Despite the fact that most researchers concur that pioneering self-viability is best comprehended as a multi-dimensional develop, regardless we locate that a great part of the exact research depends on constrained dimensional or even unidimensional proportions of ESE (Baum, Locke et al. 2001; Baum and Locke 2004; Kristiansen and Indarti 2004; Arenius and Minniti 2005). Some analyst go similarly as professing to have estimated innovative self-viability by essentially requesting that respondents answer a couple of inquiries concerning their trust in propelling another endeavor. This was as of late done in an examination by Tominc and

Rebernik (2007) were respondents needed to give a yes/no reaction to the inquiry, "Do you have the information, abilities, and experience required to begin another business?" A basic confusion, similar to the respondent feeling that she needs pertinent startup experience, before having the necessary experience to begin another business – would fill in as the reason for getting an inappropriate answer.

Multi-dimensional

Concentrates that have comprehended and attempt to quantify the more extensive Multi-dimensional nature of the pioneering self-viability build, still miss the point by depending on a "complete ESE" score Page 8 as opposed to concentrating more on the fundamental measurements (Chen, Greene et al. 1998; De Noble, Jung et al. 1999; Forbes 2005; Zhao, Seibert et al. 2005). An aggregate or composite proportion of ESE makes it difficult to recognize which measurements of self-adequacy are progressively persuasive in making pioneering expectations, if for example an elevated level of self-viability in hazard taking or the executives is of more significance than an elevated level of self-adequacy in monetary control.

The utilization of an "all out" pioneering self-adequacy score is constraining the potential effect of research did, which is obvious in the investigation by Zhao et al. (2005) that investigated the interceding job of self-viability in the improvement of pioneering expectations. They found that enterprising instruction was emphatically connected to more significant levels of pioneering self-viability, and it was likewise detailed that more elevated levels of innovative self-adequacy made a positive commitment to pioneering aims. Which is intriguing since it affirms the advantages of innovative training. Be that as it may, the utilization of a composite enterprising self-viability score makes it difficult to recognize which territories of instruction and preparing that are best in fortifying pioneering self-adequacy (McGee, Peterson et al. 2009).

The multi-dimensional nature of the pioneering self-viability build was exactly affirmed by Mueller and Goic (2003), finding that person's degree of innovative self-adequacy differed by every one of the four periods of the endeavor creation process model (looking, arranging, marshaling and actualizing). The four-stage adventure creation process model proposed by Stevenson, Roberts and Grousbeck (1994) was adjusted, developing a different proportion of enterprising self-viability for explicit undertakings related with each stage.

Another study concentrating on the basic measurements of the innovative self-viability develop in a disaggregated way was directed by Barbosa et al. (2007), analyzing the connection between subjective styles and four task-explicit kinds of pioneering self-viability. They found that that the fundamental measurements (opportunity-distinguishing proof self-adequacy, relationship self-viability, administrative self-adequacy and resistance self-adequacy) may have individual and inconsistent connections to various ward factors, specifically enterprising aims and incipient conduct.

2.9. RESEARCH FINDINGS ON WOMEN ENTREPRENEURS

V. Krishnamoorthy and R. Balasubramani (April 2014), recognized the significant ladies innovative motivation factors and its effect on pioneering achievement. The investigation distinguished desire, aptitudes and information, family support, market opportunities, autonomy, government appropriation and fulfillment are the important entrepreneurial persuasive variables. The examination additionally reasoned that _ambition', _knowledge and skill', _independence' measurements of innovative inspirational has noteworthy effect on entrepreneurial achievement.

G. Palaniappan, C. S. Ramanigopal, A. Mani (19 March 2012) in their article broke down that ladies have been effective in breaking their obstructions inside the points of confinement of their homes by going into differed sorts of experts and administrations. Ability, information and versatility in business are the principle explanations behind ladies to rise into business adventures. This examination had additionally been done to break down the persuasive components and different variables that impact ladies to become business people, the significant quality and shortcoming of ladies business visionaries and the ecological chances and dangers which advance the enterprise, and to offer recommendations to advance ladies business of chose areas in Tamilnadu. This investigation reasoned that because of absence of preparing and instruction they are not ready to get by in the market. Money is likewise the serious issue for ladies business visionaries.

Anita Tripathy Lal's (November 15, 2012) main goal of this exploration was to ponder the huge ascent of Women Entrepreneurs in India and how it has developed since the pre-autonomy days (before 1947), during the British pilgrim days. The examination additionally dissected the reasons that have incited the ladies business visionaries to release their pioneering energies into new companies. In light of both subjective and quantitative examinations the development of ladies business enterprise in India have been considered into four unique periods - Pre-Independence Period (before 1947), Post-Independence Period (after 1947),

Post-Liberalization Period (after 1991) and Post - Global Recession period (2008 onwards). The examination at last closed to what degree the different emotionally supportive networks in India can additionally encourage a helpful biological system for the Women Entrepreneurs in India.

The multi-dimensional nature of the enterprising self-viability build was observationally affirmed by Mueller and Goic (2003), finding that person's degree of innovative self-adequacy changed by every one of the four periods of the endeavor creation process model (looking, arranging, marshaling and actualizing). The four-stage adventure creation process model proposed by Stevenson, Roberts and Grousbeck (1994) was adjusted, building a different proportion of innovative self-adequacy for explicit errands related with each stage.

Another study concentrating on the fundamental measurements of the innovative self-viability build in a disaggregated way was led by Barbosa et al. (2007), looking at the connection between psychological styles and four task-explicit kinds of enterprising self-adequacy. They found that that the hidden measurements (opportunity-recognizable proof self-adequacy, relationship self-viability, administrative self-adequacy and resilience self-adequacy) may have individual and inconsistent connections to numerous needy factors, specifically enterprising goals and early conduct.

Cohoon, Wadhwa and Mitchell (2010) exhibited a point by point investigation of men and ladies business person's inspirations, foundation and encounters. This investigation recognized top five monetary and mental components propelling ladies to become business visionaries. These are want to manufacture the riches, the desire to underwrite possess business thoughts they had, the intrigue of startup culture, a long standing want to claim their very own organization and working with another person didn't offer them. The investigation reasoned that the ladies are especially worried about ensuring scholarly capital than their partner. Tutoring is essential to ladies, which gives consolation and budgetary help of colleagues, encounters and very much created proficient system.

Dr. Sunil Deshpande & Ms.Sunita Sethi, Shodh, Samikshaaur Mulyankan (Oct.-Nov.- 2009) in their exploration paper exhibits the empowering and demoralizing elements in an endeavor and to give answers for the different issues looked by the ladies business person gathering. For the improvement of ladies business person underscore ought to be on teaching ladies strata of populace, spreading mindfulness and cognizance among ladies to surpass in the endeavor field, causing them to understand their qualities, and significant situation in the general public and the incredible commitment they can make for their industry just as the whole economy.

Veena S. Samani, (2008) in her proposition illuminated a particular segment of average workers – the ladies occupied with nourishment handling. The examination shows that larger part of ladies in Gujarat have ability and extraordinary aptitude of planning and handling nourishment. The nourishment preparing might be of various kinds and amount, yet these endeavors have been seen as incredible achievement whether joined with home or not. The present examination likewise illuminates their insight, mentality and practices and issues. Stress was the serious issue looked by all the chose ladies. The specialist found that, the vast majority of the ladies business person were Hindus, around 65% of ladies had a place with family units and modest number of ladies had acquired conventional preparing.

Singh, Surinder Pal, (2008) in this examination distinguishes the reasons and impacting factors behind passage of ladies in business enterprise. He referenced the deterrents in the development of ladies business enterprise are for the most part absence of connection with effective business people, social un-acknowledgment as ladies business people, family obligation, sexual orientation separation, missing system, low need given by financiers to give credit to ladies business visionaries. He proposed the healing estimates like advancing smaller scale undertakings, opening institutional edge work, anticipating and destroying to develop and bolster the victors and so on.

Lall, Madhurima, and Sahai Shikha (2008) distinguished Psychographic factors like, level of duty, innovative difficulties and future arrangement for extension, in light of statistic factors. The examination recognized entrepreneur's qualities as self-recognition confidence, Entrepreneurial force and operational issue for tentative arrangements for development and extension. The investigation proposed that however, there has been significant development in number of ladies picking to work in family possessed business yet regardless they have lower status and face increasingly operational difficulties in running business.

Binitha. V. Thampi (January 2007) in his proposal endeavors to comprehend the relationship between ladies' work and kids' prosperity in a specific social setting. It likewise attempts to clarify the causal relationship of ladies' work status on youngster prosperity. It was discovered that as the quantity of exercises on the work front builds, the measure of time that moms spend on childcare diminishes. This examination shows that however maternal business doesn't bring about youngster dismalness results, it unquestionably obliges ladies in discovering exchange care courses of action just as convincing them to perform the vast majority of the work in the childcare system.

Sairabell Kurbah, Martin Luther (2007) in their article researched the multi-factorial nature of ladies' job in financial improvement in the East Khasi Hills territory of Meghalaya state, to decide the empowering and compelling components related with effective business enterprise as far as close to home, social, social, political and monetary qualities. Not with standing normal training and humble family foundations, the Khasi ladies have been equivalent to men in being very ambitious and effective, through difficult work, tolerance, and great advertising. Khasi culture is in certainty a solid impact in advancing such suffering characteristics among ladies, who have had the option to construct a financial base sufficiently able to furnish their youngsters with a decent beginning stage throughout everyday life. A more significant level of instruction and employable aptitudes for ladies business visionaries can help in improving their degrees of efficiency, and advance hazard taking and ingenuity.

Purnamita Dasgupta (2005) uncovered that ladies' work power investment rate in provincial India was contrarily affected by training, responsibility for, age and number of youthful (beneath 5 years) in family. Month to month per capita use contrarily influenced the choice to take an interest in the work power and was of more noteworthy essentialness for BPL families. Likewise, wage rate negatively affected ladies' work power support, however was noteworthy for BPL families.

P.K. Bardhan's (1979) dissected the determinants of ladies' work power support rate in provincial West Bengal (Indian state). He observationally demonstrated that ladies' work power support rate in country West Bengal was contrarily affected by increment in number of wards in the family unit, number of grown-up guys in the family, the town joblessness rate and way of life for the family. Ladies' work power investment rate was decidedly influenced by the collecting transplanting season (July-September). He likewise discovered that low station and innate ladies partake more in the work power than higher rank ladies even in rustic regions.

Jacob Mincer's (1962) laid accentuation on deciding components influencing of ladies' (especially wedded) choice to partake in the work power. Mincer demonstrated that spouses were bound to partake in the work power if husbands' profit were lower than lasting income. In addition, if the training level of family head was high, changes in perpetual and short lived pay feebly influenced support rate. It was likewise noticed that joblessness and nearness of small kids in families affected work power investment, however measurable importance was missing. Mincer acquainted the key determinants with ladies' work power support that could be later read for various gatherings (non-wedded or separated from ladies).

Gurendra Nath Bhardwaj, Swati Parashar, Dr. Babita Pandey and Puspamita Sahu in this examination uncovered the significant obstacles that the ladies face during beginning and running an organization for the most part originate from financing and adjusting of life. The other obstructing outside components incorporate sexual orientation separation, detachment to data, preparing openings, foundation and so on. Some inside variables like hazard avoidance by ladies, absence of certainty, absence of vision of key pioneer and so forth can likewise make impediments for the ladies enterprise advancement. This investigation proposed that administration should set a few needs for ladies business people for assignment of mechanical plots, sheds and different civilities, and careful steps ought to be embraced to maintain a strategic distance from the abuse of such office by the men for the sake of the ladies.

S. Vargheese Antony Jesurajan and S. VargheesPrabhu in their experimental examination, uncovered the desires for ladies business visionaries in Tirunelveli locale. The discovering portrays numerous components like money, preparing, backing and plans are the significant desires among the ladies business people in Tirunelveli region. The examination presumes that the ladies business enterprise must be shaped appropriately with pioneering qualities and aptitudes to meet the adjustments in patterns, challenges worldwide markets and furthermore be skilled enough to support and make progress toward greatness in the innovative field.

CHAPTER THREE

METHOD

Research method can be defined as the process the researcher follows to realize planned study's aims and objectives. It is also used to provide a foundation for the sequence of reasoned decisions that need to be made to establish how the study will be conducted. In addition, research methodology will define a number of essential elements that must be considered by the researcher to be able to progress their study, including decisions regarding overall research approach, techniques to be used for data collection, and the methodology for data analysis (Collis & Hussey 2009, p.71). Different types of research require differing approaches to data collection, and this chapter will provide an outline and justification for the approaches and methods chosen for this study, in order to achieve the identified research aims and objectives. The research approach and methods discussed in the rest of the chapter are therefore selected specifically as appropriate to an accurate understanding of the present study.

3.1. Research Design

A descriptive design is considered appropriate to the present research, because accurate and original description is needed in order to identify the factors facing women entrepreneurs. Creswell (2003) gives more detail on the nature of descriptive research, saying that a number of different factors are required to characterize it. First, such an approach is limited fact collection, but does not of necessity seek to explain why the reality described appears as it does. Therefore descriptive research does not need to look to formulate hypotheses or propose new theories. Second, descriptive research is also characterized by objectivity – descriptive research seeks to describe the reality of how a phenomenon really is. This distinguishes it from prescriptive research, an approach that is based on a concept of how reality ought to be. Finally, at the extreme end of the scale, pure descriptive research generates a collection of descriptions in a standard form without drawing conclusions, which is left to scholars in other disciplines or the reader. Nevertheless, as Grobbee (2004) noted, in the practical application of descriptive research there is a continuum of approaches from pure description through to detailed analysis, and the analysis itself may range from interpretation through to evaluation. This is also related to the degree of objectivity in the study, recognizing that interpretation and analysis of data cannot in practice be totally objective. However objective the intention is, human beings always introduce biases into their studies, and the researcher needs to acknowledge this.

Descriptive research may be designed to use multiple methods to achieve its objectives; typical techniques include naturalistic observation, surveys, interviews and case studies, in any combination. In this study, utilizing a descriptive design, the researcher adopted a survey and a series of interviews as the research tools to answer the research question and satisfy the overarching objectives of the research study.

3.2. Participants

The target population of the present study are women entrepreneurs from different enterprisers in Andhra Pradesh. Since the study focus on women entrepreneurs, the sample of this study comprises of women from two different enterprisers in the state .The population of women entrepreneurs for this study included all women entrepreneurs in the manufacturing and services sector registered under the Small and Medium Industries Development Corporation (SMIDEC). A simple random sample was taken from each state listed as members in the SMIDEC's directory. The random selection of sample was done without replacement to avoid choosing any member of the population more than once. The samples were selected from the manufacturing, services and agricultural category. The women entrepreneurs from the three sectors were engaged in diverse business activities. In the manufacturing sector, the business ranged from manufacturing of food products, textiles, handicrafts, leather accessories, chemicals, industrial components and so on. In the services sector, women entrepreneurs were engaged in beauty or bridal parlors, spa centers, computer servicing, travel agencies and marketing research agencies. In the agricultural sector, the enterprises were based on crops, livestock and fisheries. The sample for this study consisted of 104 entrepreneurs (Female-104) was randomly selected from different enterprisers in Andhra Pradesh.

3.3. Instrument

The primary data were collected through mail survey using a self-administered questionnaire. This method was deemed most practical due to the geographically dispersed samples involved in this study. To answer the research questions developed, three main parts were used demographic information. The **self-efficacy scale** and the **World Health Organization Quality of Life** have been developed specifically for the purpose, the items for which were designed based on substantiation from previous research. The standardized instruments utilized for the present study are the following:

I. Occupational self-efficacy scale (OSES):

The scale developed by Sanjot, P., Sushama.C. & Upinder Dhar. It consists of 19 items and classified into six factors like Confidence, Command, Adaptability, Personal effectiveness, Positive attitude and Individuality. The (odd-even) reliability of the scale was determined by calculating reliability coefficient, corrected for full length for a sample of 220 subjects. The reliability coefficient of the scale is .98. Besides face validity, as all items in the scale are concerned with the variable in focus, the scale has high content validity. It is evident from the assessment judges/experts that items of the scale are directly related to the concept of self-efficacy.

II. The World Health Organization Quality of Life (WHOQOL-BREF):

Quality of life assessment instrument (WHOQOL) was developed by World Health Organization, in the year of 1998. The WHOQOL-100 assesses individuals' perceptions of their position in life in the context of the culture and value systems in which they live and in relation to their goals, expectations, standards and concerns. It was developed collaboratively in some 15 cultural settings over several years and has now been field tested in 37 field centers. It is a 100-question assessment that currently exists in directly comparable forms in 29 language versions. Statistical reduction of items led to the selection of 24 specific facets and one general facet, with four items included per facet. Although there is support from exploratory and confirmatory factor analysis for the six domain structure, there is some evidence that a four domain solution may be more appropriate. However, the structure that will continue to be used for the WHOQOL-100 is the original six domain one (WHOQOL, 1998).

The WHOQOL-100 allows detailed assessment of each individual facet relating to quality of life.

In certain instances however, the WHOQOL-100 may be too lengthy for practical use. The WHOQOL-BREF Field Trial Version has therefore been developed to provide a short form quality of life assessment that looks at Domain level profiles, using data from the pilot WHOQOL assessment and all available data from the Field Trial Version of the WHOQOL-100.

Twenty field centers situated within eighteen countries have included data for these purposes. The WHOQOL-BREF contains a total of 26 questions. To provide a broad and comprehensive assessment, one item from each of the 24 facets contained in the WHOQOL-100 has been included. In addition, two items from the Overall quality of Life and General Health facet have been included. Questions should appear in the order in which they appear in the example WHOQOL-BREF provided within this document, with instructions and headers unchanged.

Questions are grouped by response format. The equivalent numbering of questions between the WHOQOL-BREF and the WHOQOL-100 is given in the example version of the

WHOQOL-BREF to enable easy comparison between responses to items on the two versions. The WHOQOL-100 field test permitted centers to include national items or facets that were thought to be important in assessing quality of life. Where centers wish to include additional national items or modules to the WHOQOL-BREF, these should be included on a separate sheet of paper and not scattered amongst the existing 26 items.

WHOQOL

Domain and Facets incorporated within

1. Physical Health

Activities of daily living

Dependence on medicinal substances and medical aids

Energy and fatigue

Mobility

Pain and discomfort

Sleep and rest

Work Capacity

2. Psychological Health

Bodily image and appearance

Negative feelings

Positive feelings

Self-esteem

Spirituality / Religion / Personal beliefs

Thinking, learning, memory and concentration

3. Social relationships

Personal relationships

Social support

Sexual activity

4. Environment

Financial resources

Freedom, physical safety and security

Health and social care: accessibility and quality

Home environment

Opportunities for acquiring new information and skills

Physical environment (pollution/noise/traffic/climate).

Participation in and opportunities for recreation/leisure.

Transport

Validity:

The WHOQOL-100 discriminated between ill and well respondents on all six domains. Largest differences between these groups were found for the level of independence domain, with scores on average 18.5% lower for ill subjects than for well subjects, compared with the environment domain where differences between groups were in the region of 5%.

Reliability:

Internal consistency

Cronbach alpha values for each of the six domain scores ranged from .71 (for domain 4) to .86 (for domain 5), demonstrating good internal consistency .Cronbach alpha values for domains 1 and 4 should be read with caution as they were based on three scores rather than the minimum four generally recommended for assessing internal reliability.

Test-Retest Reliability

Data used to assess test-retest reliability included a majority of well subjects (87% of respondents) from four centers participating in the field trial of the WHOQOL-100. These were Bath (n=90), Harare (n=100), Tilburg (n=116) and Zagreb (n=85). In all centers, respondents were university students, with the exception of Harare, where subjects were random samples of ill (n=50) and well (n=50) respondents. The interval between test and retest ranged from 2-8 weeks. Correlations between items at time points one and two were generally high, ranging from .68 For the Safety facet to .95 for Dependence on Medication. This suggests that the WHOQOL-100 produces comparable scores across time in cases where no interventions or life-altering events have occurred. However, more test-retest reliability data need to be collected for the measure.

Demographic Variables

The demographic variables included in the present study are Age, Marital Status, Education, Type of Industries, Type of Business and Years of established among entrepreneurs.

- Age: Age consists of below 30 years, 31 to 40 years, 41-50 and 51& above years.
- Marital status: Married, Unmarried, Separate and Widowed.
- Education: Below intermediate, Degree ,Post-graduation and PhD
- Type of industries: Cottage, Small scale and Large scale
- Type of business: Food, Garments, Natural, Health, Paper and Fabrication
- Years of established: Below 10 years, 11-20 years and 21 &above years

3.4. Procedures

To obtain permission for conducting the study, an official letter was secured from the research director from the Department of Psychology and the researchers' office. The researcher was approached the concerned heads to seek informed consent. After seeking permission, the target group were informed and given explanation about the purpose of the study. They were also informed that their responses will be kept highly confidential and will be used for research purpose only. Take this under the heading population just before sampling. The data was collected from different entrepreneurs of Andhra Pradesh State. Participants will be selected by the researcher using stratified sampling as the researcher focused on different women working in different sectors. The respondents approached individually and their consents sought before the questionnaires were given to them. Respondents asked to fill in their personal information before attempting to fill the questionnaires. It took thirty minutes to complete a questionnaire. The questionnaire collected as soon as each respondent finished.

3.5. Data analysis:

The analysis process will be completely presented by using Statistical Package for Social Science (SPSS) version 20 as the tools to analyze all the data collected. The analysis of collected data will be compared and constructed based on the text analysis and theory findings. Throughout the analysis process, the final part will consist theoretical part that are examined and compared with empirical findings in order to accept or generated hypothesis.

The analysis will be conducted based on different statistical procedures, such as, Mean, standard deviation, Correlation, Independent sample t- test, and one-way ANOVA. The analysis of the research will be based on the nature of the objectives presented in the research. Besides, the analysis will be carried out based on the order of the research objectives outlined in the study.

CHAPTER FOUR

RESULTS AND DISCUSSIONS

4.1 Results

This chapter presents the results and discussion in detail. To begin with, this chapter explains data screening and processing which is important for sound research followed by the sample characteristics. The statistical tests along with their suitability for the current research are outlined. In the next section, the results are analyzed and discussed in light of previously formulated hypotheses.

4.1.2. Data Screening and Processing

Processing of data began as soon as data were collected using questionnaires. The Following processes were involved in the data screening process:

Screening

Screening was done by checking for completeness of the questionnaires. Questionnaires were checked to determine if all the required items had entries and if they were consistent with each other.

Data coding and encoding

Thereafter, the coding was done for the purpose of identification before the scores were encoded into computer. The scoring was carried out as per the specifications provided in the user manual for each questionnaire. Data was encoded by keying in of the information from the questionnaires into the computer using the software SPSS 20.

Checking of encoded data

The encoded data was checked and missing values were obtained. Once the error was found, the correction was encoded in the computer and was subjected to checking again. The process was repeated until all the errors were corrected.

Checking for suitability of statistics (checking assumptions)

The last check in processing was the preparation of preliminary tables. Assumptions of the statistics to be applied were confirmed. The data met with all the assumptions.

Generation of results tables

Generation of final results tables was done after the data had passed through rigid checking procedures. This ensured that the data was of high quality.

Before carrying out data analysis the suitability for application of ANOVA and t test is to be checked. The assumptions of ANOVA and t test are:

1) Normality of distribution
2) Independent random samples
3) Homogeneity of variance/homoscedasticity

The term normal distribution refers to a particular way in which observations will tend to pile up around a particular value rather than spread across a range of values. It is generally most applicable to parametric statistics such as ANOVA and t test. The frequency distribution of scores of all dependent variables was analyzed.

The histograms showing the frequency distribution of the scores of dependent variable were found to be closer towards a normal distribution. To determine whether dependent variable is normally distributed for each combination of the levels Shapiro Wilk test was applied. The Shapiro-Wilk 'W' is the ratio of the best estimator of the variance to the usual corrected sum of squares estimator of the variance (Shapiro & Wilk 1965). The statistic is positive and less than or equal to one. The W statistic requires that the sample size be greater than or equal to 7 and less than or equal to 2,000 (Shapiro & Wilk, 1965). Being close to one indicates normality. P-value obtained should not be significant. The condition of normality of distribution was satisfied with regard to scores on dependent variables.

While following the procedure of random sampling in data collection as it is required for the application of ANOVA and t test, the second assumption of independent random samples was met.

In the table 'Test of Homogeneity of Variances' shows the result of Levene's Test for Equality of Variances. It tests the condition that the variances of both samples are equal, indicated by the Levene Statistic. In this statistic, a high value results normally in a significant difference. Significance value of 'F' is used to make the statistical decision about the assumptions of equal variance. The ANOVA and t test with equal variance assumed is unreliable if the assumption of equal variance is violated. When comparing groups like this, their variances must be relatively similar (Levene's test checks for this). If the significance for Levene's test is 0.05 or below, then the "Equal Variances Not Assumed" test is used otherwise "Equal Variances Assumed" test is used. In this research the significance obtained met with the assumption of equal variance, and "Equal Variance Assumed" test was used. As all the assumptions behind ANOVA and t test were satisfied by the present data, as such use of ANOVA and independent samples to test for this research are justified.

Statistical significance

The calculated value of ANOVA and independent sample t test is compared with predetermined significance value which is used to make the statistical decision.

In statistical significance testing, the null hypothesis is rejected when the p value is less than the significance level α (Greek alpha), which is often .05 or .01. When the null hypothesis is rejected, the result is said to be statistically significant. Both for ANOVA and independent samples T test if p<.05 it is regarded as significant and if p<.01 it is regarded as highly significant.

4.1.3. Characteristics of the Demographic Variables

In order to develop a better insight of the sample, a summary of demographic characteristics of the study sample is presented in Table 1. A total sample 104participants were involved in the study and the majority of participants 44 (42.3 %) in the range of 41 to 50 years as compared to 33(31.7%) in the age group of 30 to 40 years and 27 (26.0%) in the above 51 years. Small scale 81, (77.9%) and Medium scale 23, (22.1%) participants from industries. Of those participants, 67(64.4%) are Married, 16 (15.4%) belong to Widowed, 15 (14.4%) are Separated and 6 (5.8%) are Unmarried. From the total participants, 51(49.0%) are graduates, 36(34.6%) belong to postgraduate and 17(16.3%) are Up to High School. As per the type of business, 25(24.0%) participants are working in food processing, 25(24.0%) in fashion technology, 13(12.5%) in herbal products, 21(20.2%) in health care, (76.7%) in renewable energy and 13(12.5%) in paper products industry. Of the participants, 55(52.9%) are having below 10 years of experience, 39(37.5%) are having an experience between 11 to 20 years and 10(9.6%) are having 21 to 30 years of experience.

Table 1
Characteristics of Demographic Variables (N=104)

Variable		n	Percentage
Type of Industry	Small Scale	81	77.9
	Medium Scale	23	22.1
Marital Status	Married	67	64.4
	Unmarried	6	5.8
	Separated	15	14.4
	Widowed	16	15.4
Age	30 to 40	33	31.7
	41 to 50	44	42.3
	above 51	27	26.0
Education	Up to High School	17	16.3
	Graduation	51	49.0
	Post-Graduation	36	34.6
Type of Business	Food Processing	25	24.0
	Fashion Technology	25	24.0
	Herbal Products	13	12.5
	Health care	21	20.2
	Renewable energy	7	6.7
Experience	Below 10	55	52.9
	11 to 20	39	37.5
	21 to 30	10	9.6
	Self-employed	35	8.8

An independent-samples t-test was conducted to compare the quality of life scores and occupational self-efficacy for types of industry (Table 2). The result depicted that there is a highly significant difference among type of industry the participants are working and their quality of life along with significant difference in occupational self-efficacy where participants working in small scale industry showed higher mean value than medium scale industry where their significant quality of life were found in psychological health and environment sub domains (M=19.02, T=3.56 and M=29.11, T=4.01, two-tailed) respectively. The participants who showed significant occupational self-efficacy in medium scale industries where the self-efficacy sub domain of adaptability was found with higher mean value of (M=11.12, T=2.0, two-tailed).

Table 2

Results of independent samples t-test and Descriptive Statistics for type of industry and Quality of life, Occupational self-efficacy.

	Type of industry	N	Mean	T
Overall OSE	Small Scale	81	69.8500	3.56**
	Medium Scale	23	71.2300	
Overall QOL	Small Scale	81	93.6375	5.24**
	Medium Scale	23	92.6015	
Physical Health	Small Scale	81	23.5185	1.35
	Medium Scale	23	26.5107	
Psychological Health	Small Scale	81	19.0247	2.22*
	Medium Scale	23	19.0280	
Social Relationship	Small Scale	81	10.8272	0.98
	Medium Scale	23	9.8032	
Environment	Small Scale	81	29.1125	4.01**
	Medium Scale	23	27.1125	
Confidence	Small Scale	81	14.5000	1.12
	Medium Scale	23	12.3000	
Command	Small Scale	81	10.9136	1.56
	Medium Scale	23	9.3412	
Adaptability	Small Scale	81	10.9383	2.01*
	Medium Scale	23	11.1234	
Personal Effectiveness	Small Scale	81	15.2099	1.23
	Medium Scale	23	15.6145	
Positive Attitude	Small Scale	81	10.4198	1.09
	Medium Scale	23	12.2345	

A one-way between-groups analysis of variance was conducted to explore the impact of age on levels of quality of life and occupational Self efficacy (Table 3). Participants were divided into three groups according to their age (Group 1: 30 to 40 years; Group 2: 41 to 50years; Group 3: Group 3: 51years and above). Result revealed that there is a significant difference found among Age Groups of the participants and their overall quality of life along with no significant difference in occupational self-efficacy where participants of above 51 age showed higher mean value than medium scale industry where their significant quality of life were found in the environment sub domains (M= 30.65, F = 2.64).

Table 3

Results of One-way Analysis of Variance Results for Quality of Life and Occupational Self efficacy by Age Groups.

	Age Group	N	Mean	F
overallOSE	30 to 40	33	69.9697	1.65
	41 to 50	44	69.6364	
	above 51	27	70.4615	
Overall QOL	30 to 40	33	93.4848	2.35*
	41 to 50	44	92.4545	
	above 51	27	96.6538	
Physical Health	30 to 40	33	23.2424	1.71
	41 to 50	44	23.8636	
	above 51	27	23.2593	
Psychological Health	30 to 40	33	19.4848	.91
	41 to 50	44	18.7955	
	above 51	27	18.7407	
Social Relationship	30 to 40	33	10.8485	1.71
	41 to 50	44	10.5455	
	above 51	27	11.7037	

	30 to 40	33	28.6667	2.64*
Environment	41 to 50	44	28.9318	
	above 51	27	30.6538	
	30 to 40	33	14.5758	.12
Confidence	41 to 50	44	14.5682	
	above 51	27	14.9615	
	30 to 40	33	11.1515	.33
Command	41 to 50	44	10.8409	
	above 51	27	10.8148	
	30 to 40	33	11.1212	.19
Adaptability	41 to 50	44	11.1818	
	above 51	27	10.5556	
	30 to 40	33	15.3939	.18
Personal_Effectiveness	41 to 50	44	15.4545	
	above 51	27	14.8889	
	30 to 40	33	10.5455	.27
	41 to 50	44	10.3182	
Positive Attitude	above 51	27	10.2963	

A one-way between-groups analysis of variance was conducted to explore the impact of marital status on levels of quality of life and occupational Self efficacy (Table 4). Participants were divided into four groups according to their marital status (Group 1: Married; Group 2: Unmarried; Group 3: Separated and Group 4: Widowed). The result showed that there is no significant difference among the participants marital status and their quality of life along with no significant difference in occupational self-efficacy but there was a difference in their mean values, where participants widowed showed higher mean value than others where their quality of life were found in psychological health and environment sub domains. Adaptability, personal effectiveness and positive attitude where found with high mean with separated participants.

Results of One-way Analysis of Variance Results for Quality of Life and Occupational Self efficacy by Marital Status.

		N	Mean	F
overallOSE	Married	67	69.7576	.09
	Unmarried	6	51.6667	
	Separated	15	77.6667	
	Widowed	16	70.3750	
	Total	104	69.9515	
Overall QOL	Married	67	93.8333	.81
	Unmarried	6	68.8333	
	Separated	15	102.0667	
	Widowed	16	95.5625	
	Total	104	93.8447	
Physical Health	Married	67	23.3731	.88
	Unmarried	6	20.5000	
	Separated	15	24.6667	
	Widowed	16	24.1250	
	Total	104	23.5096	
Psychological Health	Married	67	19.1045	.83
	Unmarried	6	16.6667	
	Separated	15	20.5333	
	Widowed	16	18.0000	
	Total	104	19.0000	
Social Relationship	Married	67	10.8806	.50
	Unmarried	6	7.6667	
	Separated	15	11.4667	
	Widowed	16	11.9375	
	Total	104	10.9423	
Environment	Married	67	29.5303	.62
	Unmarried	6	20.3333	
	Separated	15	31.0000	
	Widowed	16	30.0000	
	Total	104	29.2816	

Confidence	Married	67	14.7121	.95
	Unmarried	6	10.3333	
	Separated	15	16.5333	
	Widowed	16	14.3750	
	Total	104	14.6699	
Command	Married	67	10.8358	.93
	Unmarried	6	8.6667	
	Separated	15	12.2667	
	Widowed	16	10.9375	
	Total	104	10.9327	
Adaptability	Married	67	10.8507	.03
	Unmarried	6	8.1667	
	Separated	15	12.4000	
	Widowed	16	11.3750	
	Total	104	11.0000	
Personal Effectiveness	Married	67	15.0448	
	Unmarried	6	11.5000	1.22
	Separated	15	17.2667	
	Widowed	16	15.8750	
Positive Attitude	Married	67	10.4030	
	Unmarried	6	7.5000	
	Separated	15	11.4000	0.98
	Widowed	16	10.4375	

A one-way between-groups analysis of variance was conducted to explore the impact of educational level on levels of quality of life and occupational Self efficacy (Table 5). Participants were divided into three groups according to their educational level (Group 1: Up to High School; Group 2: Graduation; Group 3: Post Graduation). Result indicated that there is a significant difference among participant education status and QOL where post graduates showed higher mean value followed by high schooled with respect to Quality of life. The sub domain of environment showing significantly higher mean difference in comparison with other domains of QOL (M= 100.04, T= 2.34). Though there is no significance found in overall occupation self-efficacy, yet significant different was found in confidence and adaptability where higher the education had higher adaptability and confidence (M= 15.68, F= 3.96 and M= 11.41, F = 2.61).

Table 5

Results of One-way Analysis of Variance Results for Quality of Life and Occupational Self efficacy by Level of education.

		N	Mean	F
overall OSE	Up to High School	17	68.4118	1.63
	Graduation	51	66.6863	
	Post Graduation	36	75.4571	
Overall QOL	Upto High School	17	91.2353	2.34*
	Graduation	51	90.4314	
	Post Graduation	36	100.0857	
Physical Health	Upto High School	17	23.7647	1.71
	Graduation	51	23.2745	
	Post Graduation	36	23.7222	
Psychological Health	Upto High School	17	18.5294	.92
	Graduation	51	18.3922	
	Post Graduation	36	20.0833	
Social Relationship	Upto High School	17	10.8235	1.71
	Graduation	51	10.8235	
	Post Graduation	36	11.1667	
Environment	Upto High School	17	28.1176	2.60*
	Graduation	51	28.4706	
	Post Graduation	36	31.0286	
Confidence	Upto High School	17	14.4706	3.96**
	Graduation	51	14.0392	
	Post Graduation	36	15.6857	
Command	Upto High School	17	10.7059	1.15
	Graduation	51	10.4118	
	Post Graduation	36	11.7778	
Adaptability	Upto High School	17	11.0000	2.61*
	Graduation	51	10.7059	
	Post Graduation	36	11.4167	
Personal_Effectiveness	Upto High School	17	15.1765	1.65
	Graduation	51	14.7451	
	Post Graduation	36	16.1111	
Positive Attitude				1.32
	Graduation	51	9.9020	
	Post Graduation	36	11.2778	

A one-way between-groups analysis of variance was conducted to explore the impact of type of business on levels of quality of life and occupational Self efficacy (Table 6). Participants were divided into six groups according to their type of business (Group 1: Food Processing; Group 2: Fashion Technology; Group 3: Herbal Products; Group 4: Health care; Group 5: Renewable energy and Group 6: Paper Products). Result showed that there is significance difference among participants working in different type of business and occupational self-efficacy and also significant difference in QOL. The sub domains of physical health and social relationships had significantly differed with other groups of professionals where Renewable energy workers had significant higher (M= 74.64, F= 4.63, M=1.6.67, F =2.97). Significant higher mean difference was also found with occupation self-efficacy with higher mean value of participants of food processing in personal effectiveness(M= 16.24, F=2.54).

Table 6

Results of One-way Analysis of Variance Results for Quality of Life and Occupational Self efficacy by Type of business.

		N	Mean	F
	Food Processing	25	74.6400	4.690**
	Fashion Technology	25	66.9583	
	Herbal Products	13	64.9231	
Overall OSE	Health care	21	67.9524	
	Renewable energy	7	80.8571	
	Paper Products	13	68.8462	
	Food Processing	25	100.0000	2.97*
	Fashion Technology	25	91.5417	
	Herbal Products	13	87.6154	
Overall QOL	Health care	21	88.8571	
	Renewable energy	7	106.5714	
	Paper Products	13	93.6923	
	Food Processing	25	24.7200	3.58*
	Fashion Technology	25	22.7600	
	Herbal Products	13	21.6923	
Physical Health	Health care	21	23.3810	
	Renewable energy	7	26.1429	
	Paper Products	13	23.2308	

Psychological Health	Food Processing	25	20.2800	1.22
	Fashion Technology	25	18.1200	
	Herbal Products	13	18.6154	
	Health care	21	18.6190	
	Renewable energy	7	20.8571	
	Paper Products	13	18.2308	
Social Relationship	Food Processing	25	11.8000	4.34*
	Fashion Technology	25	11.0400	
	Herbal Products	13	9.8462	
	Health care	21	9.6667	
	Renewable energy	7	11.8571	
	Paper Products	13	11.7692	
Environment	Food Processing	25	30.9600	1.23
	Fashion Technology	25	28.6667	
	Herbal Products	13	26.9231	
	Health care	21	28.1905	
	Renewable energy	7	33.5714	
	Paper Products	13	29.0000	
Confidence	Food Processing	25	15.9200	.90
	Fashion Technology	25	13.9583	
	Herbal Products	13	13.2308	
	Health care	21	14.5238	
	Renewable energy	7	17.1429	
	Paper Products	13	13.9231	
Command	Food Processing	25	11.7200	1.67
	Fashion Technology	25	10.3200	
	Herbal Products	13	10.4615	
	Health care	21	10.3333	
	Renewable energy	7	12.5714	
	Paper Products	13	11.1538	
Adaptability	Food Processing	25	11.8400	3.22*
	Fashion Technology	25	10.2800	
	Herbal Products	13	10.2308	
	Health care	21	10.6667	
	Renewable energy	7	10.7143	
	Paper Products	13	11.1538	

		N	Mean	F
Personal Effectiveness	Food Processing	25	16.2400	2.78*
	Fashion Technology	25	14.2400	
	Herbal Products	13	14.3077	
	Health care	21	15.2381	
	Renewable energy	7	14.0000	
	Paper Products	13	15.0769	
Positive Attitude	Food Processing	25	11.0400	.08
	Fashion Technology	25	9.4800	
	Herbal Products	13	10.0769	
	Health care	21	10.3333	
	Renewable energy	7	11.7143	
	Paper Products	13	10.5385	

A one-way between-groups analysis of variance was conducted to explore the impact of experience on levels of quality of life and occupational Self efficacy (Table 7). Participants were divided into three groups according to their experience (Group 1: Below 10; Group 2: 11 to 20; and Group3: 21 to 30). Result revealed that there is significance difference among participants having different work experience and occupational self-efficacy and also significant difference in QOL. The sub domains of physical health, environment and social relationships had significantly differed with other groups of professionals where people working from 11 to 20 years had significant higher mean (M= 73.6, F = 2.54). Significant higher mean difference was also found with occupation self-efficacy with higher mean value of participants of experience with 11 to 20 years in adaptability (M=11.3, F=3.12).

Table 7

Results of One-way Analysis of Variance Results for Quality of Life and Occupational Self efficacy by Experience.

		N	Mean	F
Overall OSE	Below 10	55	68.0000	2.56*
	11 to 20	38	73.6053	
	21 to 30	10	66.8000	
Overall QOL	Below 10	55	91.3273	4.32**
	11 to 20	38	98.1842	
	21 to 30	10	91.2000	
	Total	103	93.8447	

		N	Mean	F
Physical Health	Below 10	55	23.3273	1.15
	11 to 20	39	23.5897	
	21 to 30	10	24.2000	
	Total	104	23.5096	
Psychological Health	Below 10	55	18.8545	2.11
	11 to 20	39	19.2051	
	21 to 30	10	19.0000	
	Total	104	19.0000	
Social Relationship	Below 10	55	10.8182	3.12*
	11 to 20	39	11.3077	
	21 to 30	10	10.2000	
	Total	104	10.9423	
Environment	Below 10	55	28.2727	2.78*
	11 to 20	38	30.5526	
	21 to 30	10	30.0000	
	Total	103	29.2816	
Confidence	Below 10	55	14.1091	1.65
	11 to 20	38	15.3947	
	21 to 30	10	15.0000	
	Total	103	14.6699	
Command	Below 10	55	10.6909	1.11
	11 to 20	39	11.4103	
	21 to 30	10	10.4000	
	Total	104	10.9327	
Adaptability	Below 10	55	10.8000	3.52*
	11 to 20	39	11.5641	
	21 to 30	10	9.9000	
	Total	104	11.0000	
Personal Effectiveness	Below 10	55	15.1636	1.11
	11 to 20	39	15.6923	
	21 to 30	10	14.4000	
	Total	104	15.2885	
Positive Attitude	Below 10	55	10.1818	.90
	11 to 20	39	10.7692	
	21 to 30	10	10.0000	
	Total	104	10.3846	

Table 8 presented the Pearson coefficients for Quality of Life and Occupational Self efficacy with their sub domains. The result of the correlational analysis summarized in table 8 revealed the following aspects of interest. There is a high positive correlation observed in all the areas of quality of life and occupational self-efficacy which indicates that there is a high influence of occupational self-efficacy on quality of life. The domains of confidence, command, adaptability, personal effectiveness and positive attitude had highly significant positive correlation with the domains physical health, psychological health and environment at (p<0.01).

Table 8

Correlation Coefficients for Quality of Life and Occupational Self efficacy with their sub domains.

	Overall QOL	Physical Health	Psychological Health	Social Relationship	Environment
overallOSE	.937**	.881**	.914**	.160	.849**
Confidence	.922**	.879**	.877**	.207*	.863**
Command	.904**	.836**	.917**	.165	.789**
Adaptability	.892**	.817**	.905**	.148	.799**
Personal Effectiveness	.886**	.883**	.839**	.163	.814**
Positive Attitude	.887**	.760**	.904**	.152	.801**

4.2. Discussion

This study attempted to examine the quality of life and occupational self-efficacy of women entrepreneurs. In this part, discussions are presented according to the order of the results of the study. Consequently, the first part deals with quality of life and occupational self-efficacy of women entrepreneurs mean difference as a function of type of marital status, industry, age group, work experience, type of business and educational level. The second part dealt with the relations among quality of life and occupational self-efficacy with their sub domains.

4.2.1. Quality of life and occupational self-efficacy of women entrepreneurs mean difference as a function of type of age group, industry, educational level, marital status, work experience and type of business.

The test analysis of the independent sample t of the current study portrayed that there is a very high difference which is significant among type of industry the participants are working and their quality of life along with significant difference in occupational self-efficacy where participants working in small scale industry showed higher mean value than medium scale industry where their significant quality of life were found in psychological health and environment sub domains. This result implies that the type of industry have a great contribution for the women entrepreneurs quality of life and occupational self-efficacy. The findings of this study are similar with the findings of Tambunan (2009), Lisowska (2002) and Caruana, Morris, and Vella (1998).

The findings of one-way between-groups analysis of variance showed that there was significant Result revealed that there is a significant difference found among Age Groups of the participants and their overall quality of life along with no significant difference in occupational self-efficacy where participants of above 51 age showed higher mean value than medium scale industry where their significant quality of life were found in the environment sub domains. This result could imply that age will have an impact on the quality of life of women entrepreneurs. This result is consistent with (Hisrich and Brush, 1987; Watkins and Watkins, 1983), who found out age will have a contribution for women entrepreneurs.

The result of one-way between-groups analysis of variance demonstrated that there is no significant difference among the participants' marital status and their quality of life along with no significant difference in occupational self-efficacy. The results of the present study is inconsistent with the findings of Jacob Mincer's (1962).A possible explanation for this might be for the participants of the present study marital status will not affect their quality of life and occupational self-efficacy.

The result of one-way between-groups analysis of variance revealed that there is a significant difference among participant education status and QOL where post graduates showed higher mean value followed by high schooled with respect to Quality of life. The result of the current study implies that education level plays a pivotal role for women entrepreneurs' quality of life and occupational self-efficacy. This study is consistent with the findings of Dr. Sunil Deshpande & Ms. Sunita Sethi, Shodh, Samikshaaur Mulyankan (Oct.-Nov.-2009), Sairabell Kurbah, Martin Luther (2007).

The finding from one-way between-groups analysis of variance showed that significance among participants working in different type of business and occupational self-efficacy and also significant difference in QOL. The sub domains of physical health and social relationships had significantly differed with other groups of professionals where Renewable energy workers had significant higher mean. This finding implies that the type of business will have a great contribution for women entrepreneurs' quality of life and occupational self-efficacy. The results in this study is consistent with the findings of (Lee and Rogoff, 1997; NFWBO, 1999b).

The result in the present study portrayed there is significance difference among participants having different work experience and occupational self-efficacy and also significant difference in QOL. The sub domains of physical health, environment and social relationships had significantly differed with other groups of professionals where people working from 11 to 20 years had significant higher mean. This finding could imply that the more women entrepreneurs have an experience the better their quality of life and occupational self-efficacy. The result in the current study is consistent with the findings of Cohoon, Wadhwa and Mitchell (2010).

4.2.2. Correlation between quality of life and occupational self-efficacy

The result from correlational study depicted that there is a high positive correlation observed in all the areas of quality of life and occupational self-efficacy which indicates that there is a high influence of occupational self-efficacy on quality of life. The domains of confidence, command, adaptability, personal effectiveness and positive attitude had highly significant positive correlation with the domains of physical health, psychological health and environment. This finding could imply that whenever women entrepreneur have higher level of self-efficacy they will have also a better quality of life. The result this study is consistent with the studies conducted by Caruana, Morris, and Vella (1998).

CHAPTER FIVE

SUMMARY, CONCLUSSION AND

RECOMMENDATIONS

5.1. Summary

The main objectives of the present study are to examine self-efficacy and quality of life as a factor in influencing women entrepreneurs. Specifically, the current study deals with:

- Identify factors influencing women entrepreneurs

- To explore the extent of Self efficacy among women entrepreneurs of Andhra Pradesh.

- To study the extent of Quality of Life among women entrepreneurs of Andhra Pradesh.

- To examine the differences in the Self efficacy among women entrepreneurs based on demographic variables such as age, marital status, education, type of industries, and type of business and years of establishment among entrepreneurs.

The hypothesis formulated in this study were the following:

- There will be a significant difference in self-efficacy among women entrepreneurs based on demographic variables such as age, marital status, education, type of industries, type of business and years of established.

- There will be a significant difference between demographical variables such as Age, Marital Status, Education, Type of Industries, Type of Business and modify in the same way as #1. Years of established with Quality of life among entrepreneurs. There will be positive relationship between Self efficacy and Quality of life among entrepreneurs.

- A descriptive design is considered appropriate to the present research, because accurate and original description is needed in order to identify the factors facing women entrepreneurs. Creswell (2003) gives more detail on the nature of descriptive research, saying that a number of different factors are required to characterize it.

- The target population of the present study are women entrepreneurs from different enterprisers in Andhra Pradesh. Since the study focus on women entrepreneurs, the sample of this study comprises of women from two different enterprisers in the state .The population of women entrepreneurs for this study included all women entrepreneurs in the manufacturing and services sector registered under the Small and Medium Industries Development Corporation (SMIDEC).

- The primary data were collected through mail survey using a self-administered questionnaire. This method was deemed most practical due to the geographically dispersed samples involved in this study. To answer the research questions developed, three main parts were used demographic information. The self-efficacy scale and the World Health Organization Quality of Life have been developed specifically for the purpose, the items for which were designed based on substantiation from previous research. The standardized instruments utilized for the present study are the following:

- The analysis process will be completely presented by using Statistical Package for Social Science (SPSS) version 20 as the tools to analyze all the data collected. The result of independent sample t test depicted that there is a highly significant difference among type of industry the participants are working and their quality of life along with significant difference in occupational self-efficacy where participants working in small scale industry showed higher mean value than medium scale industry.

- Result from one way ANOVA revealed that there is a significant difference found among Age Groups of the participants.
- Result indicated that there is a significant difference among participant education status and QOL where post graduates showed higher mean value followed by high schooled with respect to Quality of life.

5.2. Conclusion

Based on the findings of the study the following conclusions were drawn:

The type of industry has a great contribution for the women entrepreneurs' quality of life and occupational self-efficacy.

Age will have an impact on the quality of life of women entrepreneurs

Education level plays a pivotal role for women entrepreneurs' quality of life and occupational self-efficacy.

The type of business will have a great contribution for women entrepreneurs' quality of life and occupational self-efficacy.

The more women entrepreneurs have an experience the better their quality of life and occupational self-efficacy.

Whenever women entrepreneur have higher level of self-efficacy they will have also a better quality of life.

5.3. Recommendations

Based the conclusions the following recommendations could be given:

Emphasis should be laid in enhancing the QOL while helping them to maintain their strengths and reducing weaknesses so that the individuals may continue to thrive in their communities and not just extend their lives.

Some sort of empowerment programs can be introduced specially for the women entrepreneurs.

All the stakeholders, community based organizations, non-governmental Organizations, civil society agencies, should make some joint efforts to enhance the QOL of women entrepreneurs.

Women should try to upgrade themselves in the changing times by adapting the latest technology benefits. Women must be educated and trained constantly to acquire the skills and knowledge in all the functional areas of business management. This can facilitate women to excel in decision making process and develop a good business network.

Self-help groups of women entrepreneurs to mobilize resources and pooling capital funds, in order to help the women in the field of industry, trade and commerce can also play a positive role to solve this problem.

Attempts should be there to enhance the standards of education of women in general as well making effective provisions for their training, practical experience and personality development programs in collaboration with educational institutions in order to improvise their over-all personality standards.

5.4. Suggestions for the Future Research

Based on the results of the study the following suggestions for the future research are made:

Future research may attempt to address issues through educational techniques in relation to QOL as educational techniques may generate awareness and assist in design of specific interventions in self-sustenance and in improving QOL.

 Future research may also include control groups and/or qualitative component to further explore the variables under investigation. Provide more contextual information specifically in the area of QOL.

More longitudinal designs need to be encouraged to assess the causality of QOL. The results from this study as well as those of previous ones concerning the variables of interest form the basis of future research.

The potential areas of future research include replication of the study using the conceptual framework with larger sample size further research.

REFERENCES

Ackerly, B. A. 1995. Testing the tools of development: credit programs, loan involvement and women's empowerment. IDS Bulletin, 26(3).

Aldrich, H. (1989), networking among women entrepreneurs. In O. Hagan, C. Rivchun and D. Sexton (Eds), Women-Owned Businesses (pp. 103–32). New York: Praeger.

Allen, C., Loudoun, R., & Peetz, D. (2007), Influences on work/non-work conflict. Journal of Sociology, 43(3), 219-239.

Allen, S. & Truman, C. (Eds) (1993), Women in Business: Perspectives on Women Entrepreneurs. London: Routledge Press.

ALLEN, S. and Truman C. (1993), "women in business perspectives on women entrepreneur", London: Rutledge press.

Almaz Negash (December 2006), Economic Empowerment of Women, http://www.scu.edu/ethics/practicing/focusareas/global_ethics/economic-empowerment.html.

AMINAH, A. (1998) .Women in Malaysia. Factors Affecting Performance", Journal of Business Venture, 12(4), 315-339

Anita Tripathy Lal (November 15, 2012) —Women Entrepreneurs in India - Over the Years! Fore School of Management.

Aparijita Sinha, What are the problems faced by Women Entrepreneur in India? lhttp://www.preservearticles.com/201101153366/problems-faced-by-womenentrepreneur.html

ASSAYAG, J. (1995). The Making of Democratic Inequality: Caste, Class, Lobbies, and Politics in Contemporary India. Pondicherry, India: Institute Français, Athena Theodore (1971), ―The professional Woman‖, Schenkman publishing company, Inc. Cambridge, Massachusetts. http://www.abebooks.co.uk/Professional-Woman-Theodore-Athena-EditorSchenkman/284635780/bd.

Baeva, M. (2004), Export: challenge to Bulgarian women entrepreneurs. Club of women entrepreneurs and managers. Bulgaria: Montreal.

BELCOURT, M; Burke, R.J. & Lee Gosselin, H. (1991) .The glass box Women Business owners in Canada. Background paper .Ottawa Ontario .Canadian advisory council on the status of women.

BERGER B (1991) The Culture of Entrepreneurship San Francisco: ICS Press BIGGART, N. (1988) .Charismatic Capitalism .University of Chicago Press.

BILODEAU M, Slivinski A (1996) Volunteering non-profit entrepreneurial services. J Econ Behav Organ 31(1):117–127.

Binitha. V. Thampi, (January 2007), A thesis on ―Economic Roles of Women and its Impact on Child Health and Care: A Study in Kerala.

Birley, N.C. Churchill, E. Gatewood, F. Hoy, R.H. Keeley, et al. (Eds.), Frontiers of entrepreneurship research (pp. 43–56). Wellesley, MA: Babson Center for Entrepreneurial Studies.

Birley, S. J., (1987). Britain's new enterprise programs. Journal of Small Business Management, 23(4), 6-12

Bowen, Donald D. & Hirsch Robert D. (1986), The Female Entrepreneur: A career Development Perspective, Academy of Management Review, Vol. 11 no. 2, Page No. 393 407.

Breen, J. Calvert, C. & Oliver, S. (1995), Female entrepreneurs in Australia: an Investigation of Factors Affecting Performance", Journal of Business Venture, 12(4), 315-339.

Bruni, A.G., Gherardi, S. &Poggio, B. (2004), Entrepreneur-mentality, gender and the study of women entrepreneurs. Journal of Organisational Change Management, 17(3): 256- 268.

Bruni, A.G., Gherardi, S. & Poggio, B. (2004), Entrepreneur-mentality, gender and the study of women entrepreneurs. Journal of Organisational Change Management, 17(3): 256- 268.

BRUSH, C., (1992). "Research on women business owners: Past trends, a new perspective and future directions", Entrepreneurship Theory and Practice, 16 (4), 5-30.

BRUSH, C.G., de Bruin, A., & Welter, F. (2009).A gender-aware framework for women's entrepreneurship .International Journal of Gender and Entrepreneurship, 1 (1), 8–24.

BRUSH, G. C., Bruin, A. D., & Welter, F. (2009).A gender-aware framework for women's entrepreneurship. International Journal of Gender and Entrepreneurship, 1(1), 8–24.

BUTTNER, E.H., & Rosen, B. (1992). Rejection in the loan application process: male and female entrepreneurs' perceptions and subsequent intentions. Journal of Small Business Management, 30(1), 58–65.

C. Mirjam van Praag, Peter H. Versloot, (August 2007), —What Is the Value of Entrepreneurship?.

Cannon, T. (1991), Enterprise: Creation, Development and Growth. London: Butterworth & Heinemann.

Carol Roth, —Entrepreneurship: 5 Challenges facing Women Entrepreneurs.

CARR, M., Chen, M. &Jhabvala, R. (1996).Speaking out: Women's economic empowerment in South Asia. London: IT Publications.

CINNAMON, R.G. &Rich, Y (2002) .Gender References in the importance of work and family roles: Implication for family work conflict. Sex Roles: A Journal of Research 47(12), 5231-541.

Cohoon, J. McGrath, Wadhwa, Vivek & Mitchell Lesa, (2010), The Anatomy of an Entrepreneur- Are Successful Women Entrepreneurs Different From Men? Kauffman, The foundation of entrepreneurship.

COHOON, J.M., Wadhwa V; & Mitchell, L May (2010) .The anatomy of entrepreneur –Are successful women entrepreneur different from men? Kauffman, the foundation of entrepreneurship, Kansas City, Missouri.

Cohoon, Wadhwa& Mitchell,(2010), —The Anatomy of an Entrepreneur- Are Successful Women Entrepreneur Different From Men?‖Kauffman, The foundation of entrepreneurship.

D'Cruz., N. K. (2003), Constraints on Women Entrepreneurship Development in Kerala: An Analysis of Familial, Social and Psychological Dimensions. Thiruvananthapuram, India, Centre for Development Studies.

Debra Efroymson, Buddhadeb Biswas, and Shakila Ruma (September 2007), ―The Economic Contribution of Women in Bangladesh Through their Unpaid Labor‖, Analysis and report writing, WBB Trust -Health Bridge Dhaka.

Dr. Sunil Deshpande & Ms. Sunita Sethi, Shodh, Samikshaaur Mulyankan(Oct.-Nov.-2009),―Women Entrepreneurship In India (Problems, Solutions & Future Prospects of Development)‖,(International Research Journal)―ISSN-0974-2832 Vol. II, Issue-9-10 Research Paper―Commerce & Management.

Ekesionye E. N and Okolo A. N5 January, 2012, ―Women empowerment and participation in economic activities: Indispensable tools for self-reliance and development of Nigerian society‖ [Department of Educational Foundations, Faculty of Education, University of Nigeria, Nsukka, Nigeria]. Educational Research and Review Vol. 7(1), pp. 10-18.

FABOWALE, L., Orser, B., & Riding, A. (1995).Gender, structural factors, and credit terms between Canadian small businesses and financial institutions. Entrepreneurship Theory and Practice, 19(4), 41–65.

Fairlie, Robert W. (2004), "Does Business Ownership Provide a Source of Upward Mobility for Blacks and Hispanics?" Entrepreneurship and Public Policy (ed.) Doug Holtz- Eakin, Cambridge: MIT Press.

Fay M and Williams L (1993), Gender bias and the availability of business loans. Journal of Business Venturing, 8(4): 363-376.

FISCHER, E.M., Reuber, A.R., & Dyke, L.S. (1993).A theoretical overview and extension of research on sex, gender, and entrepreneurship. Journal of Business Venturing 8, 151–168.

FISHER,J. (1998) Non Governments: NGOs and The Political Development of the Third World. Connecticut: Kumarian Press. 123- 145

Fox, J.M. (2001). Entrepreneurs Add Up to Big Business. Unpublished document.

G. Palaniappan, C. S. Ramanigopal, A. Mani(19 March 2012), ―A Study On Problem And Prospects Of Women Entrepreneurs With Special Reference To Erode Districtǁ, International journal of physical and social sciences, volume 2, issue 3 Issn: 2249-5894.

GASTIOUNIS, I. (2006), August 16.Malaysia's distant 2020 vision Asia Time

GEDALOF, I (1999). Against Purity: Rethinking Identity with Indian and Western Feminism. London: Routledge, Taylor and Francis.

Ghosh, P. & Cheruvalah. R. (2007).Indian female entrepreneurs as catalysts for economic growth and development. The International Journal of Entrepreneurship and Innovation, 8(2):139-148.

Godwin, Lindsey N., Christopher E. Stevens, and Nurete L. Brenner. (2006), "Forced to Play by the Rules? Theorizing How Mixed Sex Founding Teams

Benefit Women Entrepreneurs in Male-Dominated Contexts."
Entrepreneurship Theory and Practice 30: 623-642.

Goetz, A. M., and Sen Gupta, R. (1996),—Who takes the credit? Gender,
power and control over loan use in rural credit programs in Bangladeshl.
World Development, 24 (1).

Goheer, N. (2002), Women Entrepreneurs in Pakistan: A Study to
Understand and Improve

Green, E., & Cohen, L. (1995). Women's businesses: Are women
entrepreneurs breaking   new ground or simply balancing the demands of
'women's work' in a new way? Journal of Gender Studies, 4 (3), 297-314.

GREENE, P. G., Gatewood, E. J., & Carter, N. M. (2001). Women
entrepreneurs: Moving front and center: An overview of research and
theory. Women Entrepreneurs: Moving Front and Center, 3, 1–47.

GREENE, P.G., Brush, C.G., Hart, M.M., & Saparito, P. (1993). Exploration of
the venture capital industry: Is gender an issue? In P.D. Reynolds, W.D. By
grave, S. Manigart, C.M. Mason, G.D.

Grey, Mark A. and Maureen Collins-Williams.(2006), "A Rural Service
Provider's Guide to Immigrant Entrepreneurship. "University of Northern
Iowa.

Gurendra Nath Bhardwaj, Swati Parashar, Dr. Babita Pandey and
Puspamita Sahu, —Women Entrepreneurship in India: Opportunities and
Challenges.
www.chimc.in/volume2.1/volume2issue1/gurendranathbhardwaj.pdf

HABIB W M, Roni N N and Haque T (2005), "Factors Affecting Women Entrepreneurship in India: A Multivariate Analysis", Journal of Business Studies, Vol. 16, No. 1, pp. 249-258.

Hackler, Darrene; Harpel, Ellen and Mayer, Heike, (2008), "Human Capital and Women s Business Ownership", Arlington, Office of Advocacy U.S. Small Business Administration, August 2006, VA 22201 [74], No. 323.

HENNING, M. & Jardim A, (1978) : The Managerial Woman Anchors Press ,Garden city NY,pp.32

HENNING , M. & Jardim, A (1978) .The Managerial Woman .Anchor Press ,Garden city ,NY, p.32

HISRICH .R. D. Brush (1985) – "Women and minority enterprises: A comparative Analysis in E.B. Horn day, Frontier of Entrepreneurship Research, Wellesley C; MA, Babson college pp. 566-86.

HISRICH .R.D & .Brush, C.G. (1987). Women entrepreneurs: A longitudinal study in Churchill, Entrepreneurship Research, Babson College, Wellesley, M.A.Centre for entrepreneurial Studies, 187-199.

Hisrich R.D & Peters, M., 2002.Entrepreneurship. USA: Irwin/McGraw-Hill, 5.

Hisrich, R. & Peters, M. (1989), Entrepreneurship starting, developing and managing a new enterprise. Washington USA: Irwin Publishers.

Hisrich, R.D. & Ozturk, S.A. (1999). Women entrepreneurs in developing economy. Journal.

Hisrich, R.D. (2005). Entrepreneurship: New Venture creation.5th edition .Tata McGraw Hill, New Delhi.

HUMAN DEVELOPMENT REPORT (2007): United Nation Development Program.

JANI, N., and Pedroni, M. N. "Financing Women Entrepreneurs in South Asia: A Conversation with Nancy Barry. "Journal of International Affairs, 1997, 51 (1), 169–178. Journal of Small Business Management, 41 (3): 262-277.

Kuratko, D. &Welsch, H.P. (1994).Entrepreneurial strategy, text and cases.

Landes, D.S. (2003). The Calvert women's principle. A global code of corporate conduct to empower, advance and invest in women worldwide.

Lerner, M., C. Brush, R. Hisrich, (1997), "Israeli Women Entrepreneurs"

Maas, G. & Herrington, M. (2006). Global Entrepreneurship Monitor (GEM). South African report. Cape Town: University of Cape Town.

Mattis, M. C. (2004). Women entrepreneurs: out from under the glass ceiling. Women in Management Review, vol. 19, no. 3, pp. 154-163

McKay, R. (2001). Women entrepreneurs moving beyond family and flexibility. International Journal of Entrepreneurial Behaviour & Research, vol. 7, no. 4, pp. 148-165

Meyer, H.J. Sapienza, & K.G. Shaver (Eds.), Frontiers of entrepreneurship research (pp. 168-181). Babson Park, MA: Babson College.

Minniti, Maria and Pia Arenius.(2003). "Women in Entrepreneurship." Paper Presented at The Entrepreneurial Advantage of Nations: First Annual Global Entrepreneurship Symposium. United Nations Headquarters.

MOORE D.P. &Buttner, E.H (1997).Women entrepreneurs: Moving beyond the glass ceiling. Thousand Oaks CA Sage Publishing.

MOORE, D.P. (2003), "Women: Are You Ready to Be Entrepreneurs?" Business & Economic Review, 49 (2) 15-21.

NAFFZIGER, D. W., and Terrell, D. (1998). "Entrepreneurial Human Capital and the Long-Run Survival of Firms in India. "World Development, 1996, 24 (4), 689–696.

NIRANJANA, T. "Feminism and the Translation in India: Contexts, Politics, and Futures. "Cultural Dynamics, 10 (2), 133–146.

NORDIN, M (2005) .Women business: determinants for venturing in Malaysian SMEs. of financial and family issues. Journal of Enterprising Culture, 3(4): 445-461.

PARASURAMAN, S., Purohit, Y. S., Godshalk, V. M. &Beutell, N. J. (1996).Work and family variables, entrepreneurial career success, and psychological well-being. Journal of Vocational Behavior, 48, 275-300.

RAJANI N. (2008), "Management Training Needs of Women Entrepreneurs "Journal of Anthropologist" August; 10(4): pp.277- 281.

RANI, S. (1996). Potential of income generation through small scale industries (Unpublished M.Sc. Thesis). Haryana Agricultural University, Hisar, Haryana.

ROBINSON, S. 2001. An Examination of Business Ownership by Rural and Non-Rural Men in Pennsylvania. Allied Academies International Conference. Las Vegas.

Rochín, Refugio I., Rogelio Saenz, Steve Hampton, and Bea Calo. (1998), "Colonias and Chicano/a Entrepreneurs in Rural California," JSRI Research Report #16, The Julian Samora Research Institute, Michigan State University, East Lansing, Michigan.

Roomi, M. A. and G. Parrott (2008), "Barriers to Development and Progression of Women.

SCHERE, R.F., J.S., Adams, S.S.Carley & F.A.Wiebe (1989) .Role model Performance effects on Development of Entrepreneurial Career Performance, Entrepreneurship Theory.

Schumpeter, J (2005). The theory of economic development. Cambridge Mass.: Harvard   University Press.

Sekarun, U. and Leong, F.T. (1992), Women Power: Managing in Times of Demographic Turbulence. Newbury Park, CA: Sage Publications.

SHABBIR, A., & Di Gregorio, S. (1996). An examination of the relationship between women's personal goals and structural factors influencing their decision to start a business: The case of Pakistan. Journal of Business Venturing, 11(6), 507-529.

SHIM, S., & Elastick, M.A. (1993) .Characteristics of Hispanic female business owners: an expolarity study of Journal of Small Business Management's: International Council for Small Businesses.

Singh, Surinder Pal, (2008), An Insight Into The Emergence Of Women-owned Businesses as an Economic Force in India, presented at Special Conference of the Strategic Management Society, December 12-14, 2008, Indian School of Business, Hyderabad.

SINHA S. and Commuri C. (1998) "Success by Strategic Co optation: A Case Study from India." Paper Presented at the Arnova Conference, Seattle, USA. 67-73.

SRINIVASAN, R., Woo C., & Cooper, A. (1994). Performance determinants for male and female entrepreneurs. In W.D. By grave, S.

STARCHER, D. C. (1996). Women entrepreneurs: Catalysts for transformation.

STEIN, A.H., & Bailey, M.M. (1973) .The socialization of achievement orientation in female Psychological Bulletin, 80(5) 345- 366.

STONER, Charles .R; Hartman, Richard, I, 1990, Work Home Role Conflict in Female owners of Small Business: An exploratory study, 1997, Journal of Small Business Management.

SULLIVAN, P., Halbrendt, C., Wang, Q., &Scannell, E. (1997).Exploring female entrepreneurship in rural Vermont and its implications for rural America. Economic Development Review, 4, 275–300.

Tambunan, Tulus, (2009), Women entrepreneurship in Asian developing countries: Their development and main constraints, Journal of Development and Agricultural Economics Vol. 1(2), Page No. 027-040.the glass ceiling. Thousand Oaks, CA: Sage.

Timmons, J.A. et. al. (1989).New Venture Creation, Irwin, Boston.their Bargaining Power. Geneva: ILO.

Tominc, P. &Rebernik, M. (2003), The scarcity of women entrepreneurship. University of Maribor, Faculty of economics and business. Slovenia: Razlogova.

Verdaguer, M. Eugenia and Steven P. Vallas. (2008), "Barriers to Ethnic Entrepreneurship: The Latino Experience in Northern Virginia." Paper presented at the annual meeting of the American Sociological Association, New York, New York City.

Watson, J. (2003), Failure rates for female controlled businesses: Are they any different?

WHEELER, C. (1995) .Could your career use a coach? Executive Female .USA: National Association For Female Executive Inc .18 (5), 48-51.

World Bank (2007).Doing Business: How to Reform. Washington, D.C.: The International Bank for Reconstruction and Development / The World Bank.

World Bank .(2003).Importance of SMEs and the Role of Public Support in Promoting SME Development.

YOUNG, J. E. (1997). Entrepreneurship education and learning for university students and practicing entrepreneurs. In D. L. Sexton & R. W. Smilor (Eds.), Entrepreneurs 2000(pp. 215–239). Chicago: Upstart Publishing Company.

Zhou, Min. (2004), "Revisiting Ethnic Entrepreneurship: Convergences, Controversies, and Conceptual Advancements." International Migration Review 38: 1040-1074.

ACRONYMS

ANOVA	Analysis of variance
ASEC	Annual Social and Economic Supplement
BREF	Best Available Techniques Reference document
CPS	Current Population Survey
ESE	Entrepreneurial self-efficacy
GNP	Gross National Product
HR	Human Resource
MSME	Micro, small and medium enterprises
OECD	Organization for Economic Co-operation and Development
OSE	Occupational self-efficacy
QOL	Quality of Life
SME	Small and Medium Enterprise
SPSS	Statistical Package for Social Sciences
WHO	World Health Organization
WHOQOL	World Health Organization Quality of Life

Thank you for supporting me!

What Did You Think of This Book?

First of all, thank you for purchasing this book. I know you could have picked any number of books to read, but you picked this book and for that I am extremely grateful.

*I hope that it added at value and quality to your everyday life. If so, it would be really nice if you could share this book with your friends and family by posting to **Facebook, Instagram** and **Twitter**.*

If you enjoyed this book and found some benefit in reading this, I'd like to hear from you and hope that you could take some time to post a review on your favorite site. Your feedback and support will help me to greatly improve my writing craft for future projects and make this book even better.

I want you, the reader, to know that your review is very important. I wish you all the best in your future success!